Drawing from the Past

Drawing from the Past

William Weddell and the Transformation of Newby Hall

Section of the End next the Dining Room, upon the Dotted Line A.B, Mark'd on the Plan.

Leeds Museums and Galleries (City Art Gallery) in association with West Yorkshire Archive Service

Cover
Top: Section for the North Wall of the Sculpture Gallery by Robert Adam c.1767 (WYAS)
Left: Study for a plinth by William Belwood after Robert Adam (WYAS)
Right: The Sculpture Gallery at Newby Hall (photograph courtesy of Newby Hall and Jerry Hardman-Jones)
Bottom: Section showing timber framing for the Sculpture Gallery (detail) by William Belwood (WYAS)

Back Cover
A Triumphal Arch attributed to Giovanni Battista Borra, pen, ink and grey wash with pencil 43.7 x 36.7cms (WYAS, WYL5013/D/5/2/4)

Supported by the Heritage Lottery Fund, Leeds Art Collections Fund and The Paul Mellon Centre for Studies in British Art

ISBN 0 901981 69 9
Published by Leeds Museums and Galleries (City Art Gallery)
in association with the exhibition at Leeds City Art Gallery 2 November 2004–13 February 2005

Designed by FDA, Huddersfield
Printed by JW Northend Ltd, Sheffield

Photographic credits: Alex Black; The Trustees of the British Museum; Christie's Images Ltd; Jerry Hardman-Jones; Muncaster Castle; The National Trust; Newby Hall; the Trustees of the Sir John Soane's Museum; Norman Taylor; David Winpenny.

Contents

Acknowledgements

This exhibition and the accompanying publication mark the first collaboration of Leeds Museums and Galleries and West Yorkshire Archive Service. Bringing together the two services in this way allows us to share the riches of our collections with a wider public.

We should like to extend our thanks to all those who have supported this project.

Firstly, to the Heritage Lottery Fund, the Victoria and Albert Museum Purchase Grant Fund, the National Art Collections Fund, the Friends of the National Libraries, the Yorkshire Archaeological Society and the many charitable trusts and individual donors who enabled West Yorkshire Archive Service to acquire the Newby Hall Archive in 2001.

We are greatly indebted to the present owners of Newby Hall. To Mr. and Mrs. Richard Compton, Stuart Gill and the staff at Newby Hall we express our appreciation of their help and support over recent months. They have been most generous in lending items to the exhibition and in making available photographs which show their extensive renovations and careful restorations of the house, and we have benefited from their willingness to share their knowledge of Newby Hall and its owners.

Mr. and Mrs. Gordon-Duff-Pennington of Muncaster Castle and Peter Frost-Pennington have been generous lenders to the exhibition and have helped us to a greater understanding of the Weddell family.

We have relied heavily on the research and scholarly input of a number of people who have worked on the Newby Hall Archive over the years. Terry Friedman, who supervised the PhD thesis of Jill Low and guided the first catalogue of the archive from Newby, has helped in innumerable ways despite serious illness. His cheerful enthusiasm and commitment to the project has been greatly appreciated by all involved. Jill Low has kindly allowed us to use her groundbreaking research in the field and Kerry Bristol, Director of The Centre for Architecture and Material Culture at the University of Leeds, has helped us to shape the academic profile of the public programme in collaboration with Martina Droth of the Henry Moore Institute. Ruth Guilding, Eileen Harris and Martin Myrone have contributed important new thinking on Weddell and his shaping of the house and the sculpture collections at Newby. William Connor was formerly Principal District Archivist at West Yorkshire Archive Service. His essay is a fitting tribute to the major role he played in acquiring the Newby Hall Archive for the Service, and records his extensive knowledge of the whole archive, of which this exhibition and publication represents only a part.

Jennifer Alexander, on placement from Leicester University, has worked hard to bring together the public programme, while Alexandra Eveleigh and Shirley Jones from West Yorkshire Archive Service, and Victoria Worsley, Archivist at the Henry Moore Institute, have provided essential expertise in the preparation and interpretation of the exhibition.

We are also indebted to the National Portrait Gallery and the West Cumbria Record Office, particularly Robert Baxter, for their assistance.

Finally, we are indebted to those who have helped with the funding of this exhibition and the publication. The Heritage Lottery Fund have helped to extend the range of the public programme, while the Leeds Art Collections Fund and The Paul Mellon Centre for Studies in British Art have provided funding for the publication. We very much hope that the endeavours of West Yorkshire Archive Service and Leeds Museums and Galleries will lead to a sustainable working relationship that will help promote the extraordinary contribution that Newby Hall has made to the heritage of our region.

Corinne Miller
Senior Curator, Leeds Museums and Galleries

Sylvia Thomas
County Archivist, West Yorkshire Archive Service

Illustrations

Preface

The acquisition by West Yorkshire Archive Service of the Newby Hall collection of about 500 architectural drawings in 2001 was an important event in architectural history. Outstanding in both national and local terms, it includes works by architects of the quality of Robert Adam, Sir William Chambers and William Burges but its focus is local, or more accurately familial. We are used to complex collections of family papers. Comparable collections of architectural drawings are unusual.

The Newby Hall papers bring together the drawings of the Weddell, Vyner, and Robinson families which came into the possession of the Compton family at Newby Hall. It is a complex collection, not least because the families owned not only Newby Hall but also Newby Park, two Yorkshire houses whose proximity has always caused confusion. The bulk of the collection refers to these two houses but its contents range much further to include the Vyner house at Gautby in Lincolnshire and the Robinsons' London house, Grantham House in Whitehall. When read in conjunction with the more conventional family archives from Newby Hall, it presents a fascinating insight into successive generations of architectural enthusiasts.

One of the reasons why the collection is valuable is that it includes not only the work of leading London architects such as Adam, Chambers and Burges, but important local figures like William Belwood, as well as two generations of keen amateurs in the Robinson family, the 2nd and 3rd Lords Grantham. The latter, subsequently Earl de Grey, was first president of the Society of British Architects. It is a true cross-section of architectural practice, ranging from presentation to working drawings.

Though the collection was deposited briefly at West Yorkshire Archive Service, photographed and catalogued by Jill Low, it has remained largely inaccessible, and so underappreciated. The point of this exhibition is to bring the collection firmly to the attention of the public and scholars. This catalogue sets out to provide a context for the collection and in particular to focus on William Weddell, whose transformation of Newby Hall to the designs of Robert Adam still dominates that house.

Giles Worsley

William Weddell – a biographical note

In many ways, William Weddell (1736–1792) (figure 1)[1] of Newby Hall was a typical descendant of those members of the middle classes whose families had achieved wealth through trade, political status by the purchase of land and the power that this conveyed, and personal consequence by marriage into the aristocracy.[2] For a man in Weddell's position, a fashionable house and suitable collections were the outward signs of status and ambition; the country seat was the symbolic centre of his power base and its adornment was a deliberately self-conspicuous display of wealth and taste. What sets Weddell apart from most of his contemporaries, however, is the importance of his collections and the distinction of the patronage celebrated in this exhibition.

Weddell's lineage reveals a confusing repetition of Christian names, a complex series of marriages into other Yorkshire families, and a bewildering number of marriages between cousins. Indeed, for every marriage 'out', there were one or more marriages 'in'. The earliest recorded member of the family was Robert Weddell, a York butcher

Figure 1
Portrait of William Weddell, by Pompeo Batoni, oil on canvas, 1760, 234 x 183cms (courtesy of Newby Hall)

Figure 2
The South Front, Newby Hall (courtesy of Newby Hall and Jerry Hardman-Jones)

who obtained his freedom in 1511 and entered the Corpus Christi Guild in 1513.[3] His son, grandson and great-grandson, all named John, followed the same trade and were each Sheriff of York, the last being succeeded in 1599 by his brother Leonard, who also inherited lands in Clifton from an uncle, another butcher named William Drewe.[4] Leonard's second son was William Weddell of Earswick, who was sent to Gray's Inn in 1617 and married the sister of Sir John Lister. In 1650 their son, another William, married Margaret, daughter of Sir William Robinson of Newby Park and Frances Metcalfe of Nappa. Of their children, Margaret married a grocer named Alexius Elcock and Dorothy married an apothecary named Joseph Tomlinson. The children of these two unions, Richard Elcock and Barbara Tomlinson, were themselves married in York Minster in 1725. They had four children of whom three, Margaret, Thomas, and William, survived infancy. Barbara Elcock (*née* Tomlinson) is a shadowy figure but she appears to have suffered from the same mental and physical lassitude as her daughter later did and the management of her children's affairs was taken out of her hands in 1742.[5] Like most of her gender, Margaret Elcock was educated at home, but Thomas and William were sent as boarders to Ripon until 1747,[6] when their great-uncle Thomas Weddell of Earswick took the boys to London and placed them at Hackney School.[7]

The Elcocks seem to have been satisfied with the comfortable circle of York merchants and tradesmen in which they moved but Thomas Weddell was more ambitious. Having secured power and influence as Paymaster to the Navy under his fellow Yorkshireman and cousin-by-marriage, John Aislabie of Studley Royal,[8] and a large fortune made from speculating in South Sea Stock, Weddell was determined to buy his family's way into the ranks of the landed gentry. Throughout the century a symbiotic relationship existed between land and trade,[9] but socially ambitious men like Thomas Weddell looked to landownership as a source of secure income and as the means by which a man could enhance his position and his family's potential because, of course, it conveyed the control of votes, political power, and the opportunity to enter the circles of influential men.[10] This, in turn, could lead to the receipt of patronage, preferment, and public office, opening up further opportunities for amassing a fortune with which to purchase yet more land. Naturally enough, all this was cloaked with a constitutional ideology that, by limiting the power of both king and common people, concentrated it in the hands of those thought most fitted to wield it because of their stake in the land itself.[11]

Thomas Weddell was also keen to hold his extended family together and he encouraged the friendship between Richard Elcock and Thomas Robinson, the son of his cousin Sir William Robinson of Newby Park,[12] and between Elcock and his Metcalfe relations.[13] His will reflected this preoccupation. As the last of the male line of Weddell of Earswick, he laid down a complicated series of entails by which his property was to go first to Richard Elcock and his male heirs; secondly to another branch of the family, Charles Weddell of Waddow and his male heirs; then to Thomas Metcalfe of Nappa; and finally to Thomas Robinson and his heirs. All beneficiaries were to take the name of Weddell and such money as remained after the payment of debts and legacies was to be used for the purchase of land.[14]

Conspicuous by their absence are any female members of the family, excluded perhaps because the women who married 'in' would already be looked after but more likely because legacies for investment in land given to those who married 'out' would serve only to divide and reduce the family's combined wealth. No doubt this will seems unnecessarily controlling and detailed to modern readers yet, when all the other entails had failed, Thomas Philip Robinson, 3rd Baron Grantham, inherited William (Elcock) Weddell's estate thus uniting (amongst others) the properties of Newby Hall and Newby Park. This, however, is to get ahead of ourselves.

In 1747 Richard Elcock duly inherited a fortune, excluding land, of about £70,000.[15] After arranging for his uncle's funeral, he paid various legacies amounting to some £18,000 and took the name of Weddell.[16] The following year he spent £9,530 on the purchase of Newby Hall, John and Edward Blackett's estate on the River Ure between Ripon and Boroughbridge. Soon after this, he acquired more land in Gilling, Gargrave and Gisburne; the manor of Sawley; and further land in Skelton and Mulwith, adjacent to his Newby estate.[17] He also leased a London townhouse[18] and, as Eileen Harris explores elsewhere in this publication, began to think about bringing in John

Carr to alter Newby just as Carr was establishing himself as the foremost local architect of his generation and the county was experiencing a boom in the construction and alteration of country houses.[19] Meanwhile, his sons remained at school at Hackney until April 1753 when William was admitted to Gray's Inn; the law being a profession that was socially acceptable for a younger son and one capable of providing excellent opportunities for advancement. One had only to look to the example set by the Lord Chancellor Philip Yorke, first Earl of Hardwicke, and his sons to see what might be achieved. The following month both boys entered their father's old Cambridge college, St. John's,[20] matriculating at Michaelmas 1753, although neither took a degree.

Given the nature of his northern roots, it is unsurprising that the majority of William Weddell's friends and associates were Yorkshiremen, but he made a number of friends at Cambridge with whom he kept in touch until the end of their lives. The closest of these was William Palgrave, the second son of an Ipswich doctor, who took Holy Orders in 1759 and became a scholar of Pembroke College, LL.B. in 1760 and a Fellow in 1764. It was probably through Palgrave that Weddell was introduced to the poets Thomas Gray and William Mason. He was never to share Gray's delight in the gothic or Mason's radical politics, but all had a deep interest in the classical world and their names, together with those of Frederick Montagu, Jack Wheler and Norton Nicholls, recur throughout Weddell's life. One hopes that they were able to compensate, at least in part, for the sudden death of Thomas Weddell on 24 December 1756, aged twenty-two. The death of his older brother radically altered William Weddell's position; all thoughts of a legal career were set aside and he prepared to live the life of a landed gentleman. A military career was never on the cards although in 1759, in the middle of the Seven Years' War, he joined the militia, serving largely in the north of England and achieving the rank of captain.[21] This brought him into the orbit of the man who was to become his patron and mentor, Charles Watson-Wentworth, 2nd Marquis of Rockingham.

Barbara Weddell died at the end of 1761, followed within a year by her husband. The Weddells' close relationship with the Robinson family at Newby Park now became apparent as the first person William Weddell contacted after his father's death was

Thomas Robinson, now 1st Baron Grantham.[23] Richard Weddell had desired that his 'body may be decently, but in a private manner, interred in the parish church of Strensall, being the family burial place' and his son accordingly made the necessary arrangements.[24] Such matters attended to, and his sickly sister placed under the watchful eye of the Robinsons,[25] Weddell resolved to visit the Continent, no doubt encouraged by the cosmopolitan Lord Grantham, since Richard Weddell had not seen the need for such expense, and furnished with appropriate letters of introduction by Grantham's son, recently returned from his own Grand Tour.

Weddell sailed for The Netherlands on 20 August 1762 from where, after a busy month of sightseeing, he headed for Paris. Here he visited the usual buildings, gardens, and art collections and, perhaps bearing in mind the alterations at Newby Hall discussed by Dr. Harris, he may have paid a visit to the Manufacture des Gobelins to purchase the tapestries that still hang at Newby today (figure 3). However, any

Figure 3
Gobelin tapestries in the Drawing Room (courtesy of Newby Hall and Jerry Hardman-Jones)

plans to visit Italy were cut short when the Robinsons began to press him to make a new will and settle his affairs and to remind him of his duties towards his fragile sister.[26] Weddell yielded to pressure and returned home.[27] Apart from Margaret, it is not clear exactly what affairs he had to settle. Perhaps these were in connection with a claim made against Thomas Weddell's estate by a distant cousin that William dealt with in July 1764,[28] shortly before he returned to the Continent in the company of his Cambridge friend, William Palgrave.[29] Passing through France and Switzerland, they arrived in Italy in November. In Rome, Weddell sat to distinguished painters, commissioned other works of art, and amassed a notable collection of ancient sculpture which, as Martin Myrone and Ruth Guilding explore in more detail, was part of a calculated attempt to amass the external signs of class and culture while developing and displaying his unique personal taste.

Weddell came home in the summer of 1765. As a man of wealth and a substantial landowner in the region, it was perhaps a natural step for him to enter politics.[30] Being from a newly-landed family, however, he did not have access to a traditionally held ancestral seat, so it was probably necessary to be nominated for a local independent constituency, which effectively meant York or Hull. York was soon dismissed as too venal and expensive to win[31] and, in the end, Weddell turned to the Marquis of Rockingham when he decided to run for the Hull seat left vacant when Sir George Metham was appointed Clerk to the Wardrobe in 1766.[32] Metham had been the Rockinghamite member for Hull since 1757.

Rockingham's political reputation – from his teenaged attempt to join the Duke of Cumberland at Carlisle to his brief spells as prime minister and self-appointed role as heir to the Whigs of the Revolutionary Settlement of 1688 – is still the subject of intense debate between historians eager to lavish praise on the leading role he played in the development of party politics after George III's accession and those equally keen to dismiss him as turf-mad or as lacking the personal qualities necessary to make a real success of high office.[33] This need not concern us here, beyond noting that Rockingham was as active in local politics as he was at national level and that half of the MPs who supported him in the House of Commons were elected either with his direct support or the support of the Rockingham Club at York.[34] William Weddell became one such MP, typical of the Rockingham following in the House of Commons 'who appear to have entered Parliament largely to demonstrate their standing among the leading gentry families in the regions.'[35] This was reflected in Weddell's decision to remodel Newby Hall in the latest fashion long before he even thought of a London townhouse; No. 6 Upper Brook Street, close to Rockingham's townhouse in Grosvenor Square, was not acquired until after his marriage in February 1771.[36] In this he may have followed Rockingham's example, for the latter used Wentworth Woodhouse as his political power base and never lavished much wealth or attention on his London house.

Of equal importance for the future appearance of Newby Hall, 1766 was also the year in which Lord Grantham proposed Weddell for membership of the Society of Dilettanti; a convivial dining club long recognised to have included some of the most important arbiters of taste in the latter half of the eighteenth century. Within a decade, he was joined by Edwin Lascelles, Lord Mulgrave, John Smyth, Walter Spencer-Stanhope, Henry Peirse, and Richard Thompson, suggesting a regional bias in the election of new members at this time.[37] Soon after joining, Weddell turned to William Chambers and then Robert Adam to create the dramatic sculpture gallery and suite of reception rooms for which Newby is known. One wonders whether the drive to neo-classicise his house would have been as strong had Weddell possessed the spectacular wealth and political importance of Rockingham, who had been a Dilettanti since 1755 yet can hardly be said to have fallen under its architectural spell.

When the septennial general election came round in 1768, Weddell was forced to defend his seat. He was already in poor health and some of his supporters anticipated trouble,[38] but, with Rockingham behind him, Weddell was fairly confident of success. Fortunately his predictions were proved correct because he allowed his attention to be diverted towards Adam's improvement of Newby Hall instead of the otherwise necessary relentless campaigning that victory usually required. He had also begun to think of marriage. 'The marriage possibilities for the circle of people who might

own great houses were. . . tight but not impenetrable'[39] and this time it was Mary, Lady Rockingham, who stepped in to assist.

As the daughter of Thomas Bright of Badsworth and his wife Mary Norton, Lady Rockingham was a great heiress in her own right as well as her husband's trusted adviser and 'secretary' (her term).[40] Her mother had married as her second husband Sir John Ramsden of Byram Park in 1748 and their eldest daughter, Elizabeth (known as Bess), was selected to be the future Mrs. Weddell (figure 4).[41] There was considerable speculation among the Robinsons as to whether the match would come off[42] but, with the determined Lady Rockingham in charge, the outcome should never have been in doubt.[43] Apart from the political and financial desirability of the match,[44] genuine affection seems to have been felt by both parties. Before the marriage, Elizabeth informed her half-sister:

My Mind is still too much agitated by the importance of the affair I have now under Consideration, to find terms to express how much I sincerely think myself obliged to you, & Lord Rockingham for your very great kindness to me. . . from the exceeding good Character from those Friends I depend upon, & indeed from all indifferent People, & the good opinion I have myself formed of Mr. W. (which I have not had the least Reason to alter) I can't doubt of his being the person in whom I may place my Trust, & Confidence being also thoroughly persuaded that there can be no inducement on his Side but real regard, & attachment.[45]

Weddell offered his thanks to Lady Rockingham four days after the wedding.[46]

Given the important collections amassed by their respective husbands, and the state of near perpetual construction in which their country seats must have been, it is surprising that architecture and the fine arts do not feature more often in the surviving Rockingham-Weddell correspondence. This is doubly surprising when one takes into account their mutual employment of John Carr, Robert Adam, James Stuart, Joseph Nollekens, George Stubbs, and Joshua Reynolds, to name but a few – and that Elizabeth Weddell was a talented amateur artist in her own right. Lady Rockingham made a tantalising reference to Adam's work at Newby Hall in an undated letter,[47] but illness, lethal-sounding remedies, and politics occupy the bulk of her near-daily missives to her husband. Fewer Weddell letters have been preserved, but in-depth discussion of the work at Newby is also curiously lacking. This is all the more noteworthy as the opportunity to relay updates on improvements would have been provided by their frequent reciprocal visits in London and between Wentworth Woodhouse, Newby Hall, Byram Park, and Woodchester Park, the latter being the Gloucestershire seat of Lord Ducie, who married Margaret Ramsden in 1774. Perhaps such matters were stored up for discussion in person, as is suggested by another letter in which Lady Rockingham teased her husband by stating 'The News of your Purchases is as antique as your Venus: The two Weddells dined with me yesterday & told me.'[48]

Although the surviving letters between Elizabeth and William Weddell lack the passionate yearning for each other that characterises the Rockingham correspondence, messages of love and regret were exchanged whenever the Weddells were separated. No records of Mrs. Weddell's skills as a political hostess seem to have survived, but her political advice was also welcome, even if it lacked the vigour and acuity of that of her half-sister.[49]

The early 1770s were probably the high point of Weddell's life: he had just married and hoped for an heir, he had been successful at the Hull election and probably expected advancement, and his Yorkshire seat was being refurbished in a manner commensurate with his ambitions. Unfortunately, the Weddells were never to have children and the deterioration of William's political career began as early as 1774, when illness, natural modesty, preoccupation with the work at Newby, or perhaps dislike of the corruption involved, caused some local 'discontent on [his] want of activity etc'[50] after Rockingham had helped procure an Act for establishing further docks and quays at Hull. At the request of certain merchants who disliked the idleness and disorder connected with the local races, Weddell had also refused to subscribe, thereby offending another sizeable faction of voters. Rockingham tried to repair the damage[51] but Weddell had to stand down and David Hartley was put forward as a candidate in his place. Weddell was offered the safer seat at Malton made available by Edmund Burke's victory at Bristol. In Parliament Weddell supported Rockingham's policies against the war with the American colonies and in favour

Figure 5
Portrait of Captain William Weddell, by Joshua Reynolds, oil on canvas (courtesy of Muncaster Castle / Alex Black)

of reform at home. The latter was a key issue in Yorkshire where the independent gentry had formed an Association and pressed for radical changes. Among their ranks were Harry Duncombe and William Mason. The Association's main aims were to reform abuses of public expenditure – including the reduction or removal of expensive and outdated sinecures – electoral reform, and shorter parliaments. Rockingham was probably correct in his assessment of the political unfeasibility of promoting these demands but the Associates were equally percipient in interpreting his caution as a self-preserving, delaying tactic.[52] Weddell was caught in the middle and chose a curious path, opting for caution by joining with other large landowners to protect their mutual interests but proposing Sir George Savile and Harry Duncombe as candidates for the county seat at York against Edwin Lascelles[53] once his own seat at Malton was secured.

The fall of Lord North and the end of the war in America removed much of the focus of the Association's discontent although the rift with Rockingham continued to widen until the latter's sudden death in July 1782. For the Weddells, Rockingham's death was a considerable family loss and Elizabeth spent a great deal of time comforting her sister.[54] For William, it almost certainly meant the end of any hope of personal preferment. He failed to win a seat for the county of York in 1784[55] but returned to represent Malton, the seat being vacated for him by Thomas Gascoigne. Soon Weddell was feeling 'almost a disgust about every manoeuvre in the political world' and informed his wife that 'there is no comfort in politics.'[56] He continued to work with Rockingham's nephew and heir, Lord Fitzwilliam, and was again returned for Malton in 1790 but he had passed into the political wilderness even before he was incapacitated by an attack of a recurring illness.[57] He died on 30 April 1792 during a visit to the Roman Baths in Surrey Street on an exceptionally hot day.[58] It was an ignominious end for a man who never achieved the dizzy political heights to which he aspired but who, nonetheless, has a serious claim to be one of the most cultivated and perceptive patrons of his era.

The Newby Hall Drawings

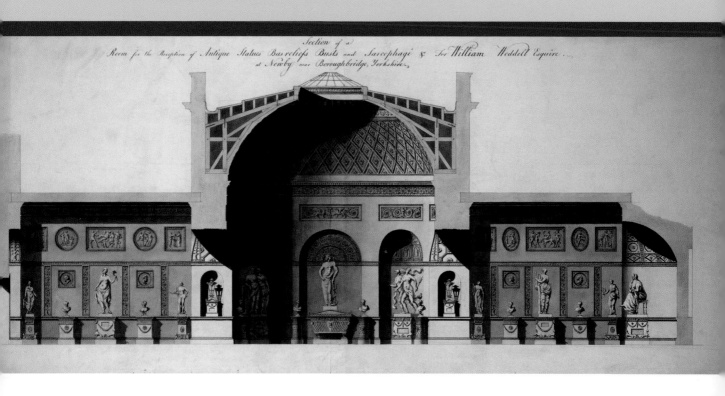

The architectural drawings from Newby Hall are a collection of about 500 items. They were purchased from Mr R.E.J. Compton by West Yorkshire Archive Service in 2001 as part of the archives of the Newby Hall Estate.[1] Most of these archives had been deposited on loan at the Leeds office of the Archive Service for many years, but the existence of these drawings, which had remained at Newby, only became apparent in the past generation or so. They relate to Newby Hall itself and a number of other houses with which this family and its predecessors have been associated over the past three centuries. The collection is remarkable not only for the work of some of the leading architects of the eighteenth century (figure 7), but also for illustrating that of others hardly represented elsewhere, such as the 2nd Lord Grantham, his son, Earl de Grey, and William Belwood, whose contribution to the architecture of Yorkshire has been brought to light by the evidence here.

We do not know when these drawings were collected together, but it seems likely to have been the work of Major E.R.F. Compton, who took over responsibility for the

Figure 6
The Sculpture Gallery, Newby Hall (courtesy of Newby Hall and Jerry Hardman-Jones)

Figure 7
West/east section of the north wall of the Sculpture Gallery by Robert Adam, pen, ink and coloured wash, 118 x 59.5cm (WYAS, WYL5013/D/1/6/12)

property from his mother in 1921 and remained in charge until his death in 1977. The first published reference to them is by Hugh Honour in 1954, but he speaks only of 'a few' drawings at Newby, including Adam's designs for the ante-room and the original library, William Belwood's plans for Newby Park at Baldersby and the drawings for Gautby in Lincolnshire by Brettingham and Lindley (figure 8). In 1966 the R.I.B.A. was able to acquire numerous Colen Campbell items from this source, but, apart from a few scholarly references, most notably by John Cornforth in 1967 and John Harris in 1970, they did not come before the world at large until they were deposited temporarily with Leeds City Art Galleries at Temple Newsam House in 1978–1979. There they were photographed for the National Monuments Record and used by Jill Low in her research for her doctoral dissertation at the University of Leeds on the artistic patronage of William Weddell. Her thesis was completed in 1981 and included an arrangement and detailed listing of these drawings, which remains the main means of reference to them.[2]

The core of the present house was built in the 1690s, about twenty years after the purchase of the estate by Sir Edward Blackett, a merchant from Newcastle-upon-Tyne, who had become MP for Ripon in 1689. The Blacketts sold the property in

Figure 8
Elevation of the east front, Gautby Hall by William Lindley, pen, ink and coloured wash, 1803, 30.7 x 53.5cms (WYAS, WYL5013/D/9/2/10)

1748 to Richard Elcock, a York merchant, who took the name of Weddell from his maternal uncle, from whom he had inherited a large fortune. On Richard's death in 1762 the estate passed to his only surviving son, William. He was a young man of twenty-six who, after a short career in the local militia, made the Grand Tour in 1763–1765. On his return home he employed John Carr, Robert Adam, William Chambers and others to make extensive alterations and additions to the house at Newby.

When William Weddell died suddenly and childless in 1792, the property passed, under the terms of his great-uncle's will, to his distant cousin, Thomas Robinson, the 3rd Baron Grantham.[3] The Robinsons had a seat of their own at Baldersby, near Thirsk, which confusingly, at this time was called Newby Park. It had been built by Thomas' great-grandfather, Sir William Robinson, to designs by Colen Campbell, and was remodelled in 1782 by the local architect, William Belwood.[4] Thomas and his father, the 2nd Lord Grantham, were themselves both keen amateur architects and, after Thomas had come into his inheritance he made alterations and additions to Newby Hall to his own designs. With the inheritance of his aunt's estate in 1833 also came the earldom of de Grey and barony of Lucas. In 1845 he sold Newby Park at Baldersby and gave Newby Hall to Henry Vyner, who had married his younger daughter, Mary.[5] The Vyners were established at Gautby in Lincolnshire and also had an estate at Bidston on the Wirral peninsula.

From this point there is only one Newby in the story, but a further complication arises from the death in 1845 of Mrs. Elizabeth Sophia Lawrence, the owner of the neighbouring estate of Studley Royal. Although never married, she was always known as Mrs. Lawrence. This property was also inherited by Earl de Grey, subject to an entail on his younger brother who, as Viscount Goderich, had briefly been Prime Minister in 1827 and became Earl of Ripon in 1833. Both Mrs. Lawrence and the Robinson brothers were descended, respectively from John Aislabie, the Chancellor of the Exchequer in 1720 and creator of the famous gardens at Studley, and from his sister Mary. This link was further reinforced by the marriage of Henry Vyner's daughter to Lord Ripon's son and her distant cousin, George Frederick Samuel

Robinson, later 1st Marquis of Ripon. This brought the two neighbouring estates of Newby Hall and Studley Royal unusually close so that, in the early twentieth century they were held by two brothers, both descendants of the marriage of Mary Robinson and Henry Vyner: Edward Compton lived at Newby and his brother Clare, who took the name of Vyner, succeeded to Studley Royal. A consequence of this is some confusion in the arrangement and survival of the archives generated by two centuries of building and estate management. Fortunately both collections are now held under one roof at West Yorkshire Archive Service in Leeds.[6]

As often happens in situations of such complexity, there are also materials elsewhere relating to the Robinson family and their connections. Apart from the Colen Campbell material at the R.I.B.A., which was acquired directly from Newby Hall and Studley Royal in 1966,[7] there are also some stray items in collections elsewhere, such as Robert Adam's design for the tapestry room ceiling amongst the Pennington-Ramsden Archives at the Cumbria Record Office, Whitehaven. This, along with William Weddell's diary of the first part of his Grand Tour and a tantalising selection of his correspondence, presumably passed through the estate of William Weddell's widow, Elizabeth, the sister of Sir John Ramsden of Byram Park, and migrated to Cumberland when the Ramsden family moved its seat from Yorkshire to Muncaster Castle.[8] The correspondence, mostly with Weddell's Grand Tour companion, the Reverend William Palgrave, and the poet William Mason, is now also held by West Yorkshire Archive Service at Leeds.[9]

The Wrest Park Archives, now at the Bedfordshire Record Office, include estate plans, family correspondence, an estimate for alterations for Sir Thomas Robinson at Whitehall c.1750, plans of Newby Park (Baldersby) 1784 and notes about work there 1786. There are also drawings attributed to Earl de Grey for his London house at 4 St James's Square and for Buckingham Palace, where he was a member of the commission set up to supervise the building of the new entrance front in 1846–1850.[10]

Other related collections are the Blackett Archives at the Northumberland Record Office, which contain material about Newby before the Weddell purchase, papers

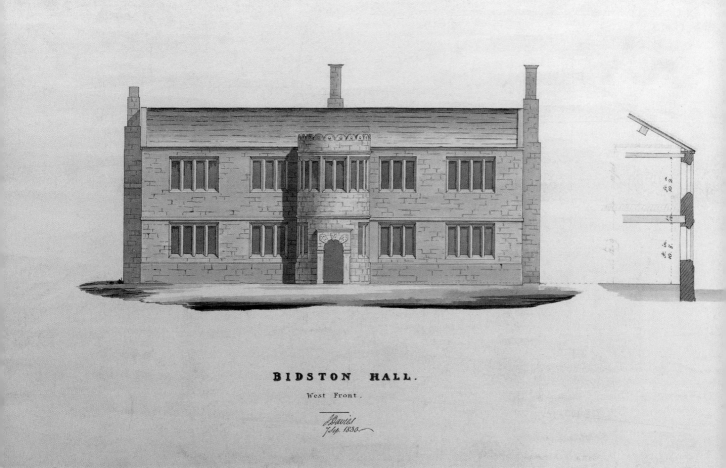

BIDSTON HALL.

West Front.

Davies
7 Sep. 1830

Figure 9
The West Front of Bidston
Hall by John Davies, pen,
ink and wash, 1830,
33 x 51.1cms (WYAS,
WYL5013/D/10/1/5)

about the Vyner family estates in Lincolnshire and Cheshire in the respective county record offices, papers about the Robinson and Weddell estates in and around York in the York City Archives and family, political and diplomatic papers of the Robinsons, formerly at Studley Royal, at the British Library.[11]

The Newby drawings fall into three main groups. First there are those relating to the house itself. Dating from about 1700, they incorporate the alterations made for William Weddell by Carr, Chambers, Adam and Belwood, by Earl de Grey for himself in the early nineteenth century and the work by William Burges for Lady Mary Vyner.[12] With these are included the designs for alterations to the house at 6 Upper Brook Street in Mayfair, which William Weddell acquired after his marriage to Elizabeth Ramsden in 1771. Secondly there are the drawings made by the 2nd Lord Grantham and William Belwood for alterations and estate buildings at Newby Park, Baldersby, between 1763 and 1785. To these may be added a series of eight drawings by William Chambers for Grantham House in Whitehall. Third is the group relating to the properties of the Vyner family, mostly for Gautby Hall in Lincolnshire, but also a few drawings of Bidston Hall in Cheshire in 1830 by John Davies (figure 9).

Figure 10
A Triumphal Arch attributed
to Giovanni Battista Borra,
pen, ink and grey wash with
pencil 43.7 x 36.7cms
(WYAS, WYL5013/D/5/2/4)

Outside these main groups there are more miscellaneous categories where, in some cases, the provenance is less clear. These include various drawings associated with the practical architectural interests of the 2nd Lord Grantham and of his son, Earl de Grey, and drawings probably made and collected by Grantham during his Grand Tour. The latter include a few originals, at least one of which is by Giovanni Battista Borra (figure 10), his drawing master at Turin. Another is a sheet containing two separate leaves of a design for a fountain by Giacomo Ciolli submitted to the Concorso Clementino in Rome in 1706, possibly copies from the archives of the Accademia di San Luca in Rome.[13] There are others associated with Grantham's time as ambassador at Madrid (1771–1779). As an enthusiastic amateur he could not resist also supplying designs for his neighbours and relatives. Thus there are drawings for garden seats at Studley Royal (figure 11) and for a chapel and round tower at Saltram in Devon, the seat of his brother-in-law, John Parker (figures 12 and 13).[14]

Figure 11 (top left)
Elevation of a wooden garden seat at Studley Royal by Thomas Robinson, pencil and grey wash, 1764, 22.8 x 20.4 cms (WYAS, WYL5013/D/5/4/1)

Figure 11 (centre)
Sketch for a garden seat at Studley Royal by Thomas Robinson, pencil, 9.9 x 16.7cms (WYAS, WYL5013/D/4/4/2)

Figure 12 (top right)
Elevation of a tower, Saltram by Thomas Robinson, pen, ink and brown wash, c.1769, 38.2 x 26.6cms (WYAS, WYL5013/D/5/5/6)

Figure 13 (bottom)
Section, plan and elevation of chapel and round tower at Saltram by Thomas Robinson, pen, ink and coloured wash 31 x 24.6 and 28.8 x 24.5cms (WYAS, WYL5013/D/5/5/1&2)

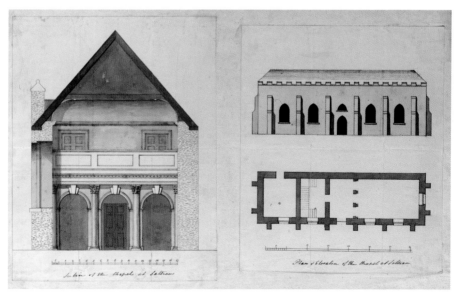

Another group of early-eighteenth century drawings has been tentatively attributed by Dr. Low to Colen Campbell and/or John Etty (figures 14 and 15). They are mostly designs for ceilings and panelled interiors and may be related to the Campbell drawings acquired by the R.I.B.A. from this source in 1966 and which, containing preparatory drawings for *Vitruvius Britannicus*, are thought by John Harris to have come from Campbell's office.[15]

The collection illustrates the wide range in style and quality of architectural drawings in general. As technical, working drawings they fall between works of art and the administrative archives which, as the product of a design and building process, they undoubtedly are. Needless to say, they do not always show the building as finally executed and need to be used in conjunction with other surviving archives, such as specifications, accounts, correspondence and estate plans, to show how the project developed on site.

The drawings fall into two categories, either as vehicles for presenting the architect's scheme to the client, or as technical instructions to the builders and craftsmen.[16] Sometimes they are both at the same time. The presentation drawings may be perspectives, showing how the completed building might look when seen from a distance in its landscape setting, or they may be measured elevations and sections,

Figure 14
Ceiling design probably by Colen Campbell and/or John Etty, pen and ink, early 18th century, 29.5 x 39.3cms (WYAS, WYL5013/D/8/1/9)

Figure 15
Laid-out wall elevations of a room, probably by Colen Campbell and/or John Etty, pen and ink, early 18th century, 42.2 x 32.5cms (WYAS, WYL5013/D/8/1/2)

finished to a high standard, with tinting and shading to indicate the fall of light. The latter will be drawn to scale and strictly two-dimensional, without the application of perspective. They may also incorporate structural details, such as floor levels or the manner of integration with adjacent buildings, which would not be part of a straightforward artist's impression. Therefore these are both presentations and technical drawings. For example, Adam's section of the sculpture gallery at Newby (figure 7) shows the structure of the dome roof, the decorative scheme of the walls and the arrangement of statues and pedestals.[17] The second purely technical category is less ambiguous, showing details of design and construction, from plaster mouldings, door cases and chimneypieces to wall frames and roof timbers.

The drawings for Newby Hall itself, particularly those for Adam's scheme, represent both categories and are unusual amongst collections of this kind in documenting the whole design project, from initial inception through to development of the details, the preparation of blank wall templates and the submission of final designs by others. In this way they supplement the records of the Adam practice at Sir John Soane's Museum to form an unusually complete picture of the commission and its execution.

Although these Adam items are the most striking, they are matched by some very accomplished and elegant designs for a number of buildings and details, formerly attributed to him, such as the plinths in the statue gallery, the stable block and the Boroughbridge gate lodges, which can now be shown, at least in final execution, to be the work of William Belwood, a local architect who worked both for Adam and on his own account. On the other hand, Sir William Chambers was accustomed to work out the details either himself or in his own office, and John Cornforth has commented that his drawings in this collection, in particular those for interior details, are the clearest of the kind which he has encountered.[18] Adam appears to have worked personally on some furnishing details, most notably for a plate warmer and the alabaster urns on stands for Weddell's dining room, now the library, which were fitted to take lights. These urns remain in the house and one can imagine the magical effect of the light they would have produced when lit by candles or oil lamps, without the competition of electricity. There were no ceiling lights, and so the room would

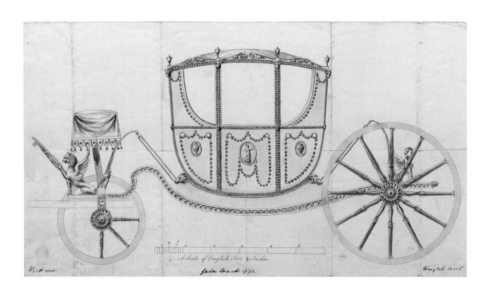

Figure 16
Design for a State Coach by
James Wyatt, pen, ink and grey
wash, 1775, 40 x 56cms
(WYAS, WYL5013/D/3/1/14)

have acquired some of the dramatic atmosphere of a Piranesi print, an effect enhanced by moving into the adjacent sculpture gallery, where lighting from lamps at a low level was also in place.[19] Adam was also consulted about alterations to Weddell's London house at 6 Upper Brook Street but, when eventually carried out in the 1780s they were to designs by Samuel Wyatt, with interiors by him and the younger Chippendale.[20] Along with the drawings for this work may be associated one attributed to Samuel's brother, James, for a state or gala coach such as, even in this age of conspicuous consumption, would only be commissioned by a grandee (figure 16).[21]

The drawings for outbuildings are also of unusual interest. There are those, possibly by Elizabeth Weddell, for decorating the farmhouse at Newby where, we may suppose, she played at rustic pursuits in the manner of Marie Antoinette (figures 17, 18 and 19).[22] Her friend, Miss Hartley, supplied a drawing for the eagle to go above the porch of the new front door to the Hall itself.[23] The 2nd Lord Grantham designed a pedimented 'root house' of timber log construction at Baldersby (figure 20)[24] and his son, the later Earl de Grey, did drawings for an ice house at Newby.[25] The latter, alongside his career as a statesman culminating in his appointment as viceroy of Ireland 1841–1844, was the first president of the Society of British Architects

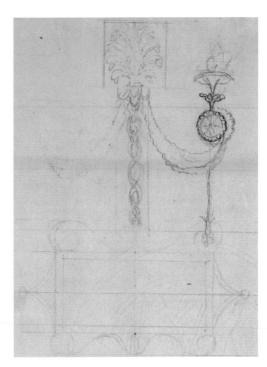

Figure 17 (top left)
Design for decoration for
the farmhouse by Mrs.
Elizabeth Weddell, oil paint,
37.5 x 36cms (WYAS,
WYL5013/D/1/21/5)

Figure 18 (below top left)
Design for decoration for
the farmhouse by Mrs.
Elizabeth Weddell, oil paint,
21.9 x 55.4cms (WYAS,
WYL5013/D/1/21/4)

Figure 19 (top right)
Designs for wall decoration
for the farmhouse by Mrs.
Elizabeth Weddell, pencil,
32 x 20cms (WYAS,
WYL5013/D/1/21/2)

Figure 20 (bottom)
Drawing of the Root House
by Thomas Robinson, pen,
ink and coloured wash, 1785
(WYAS, WYL5013/D/4/2/13)

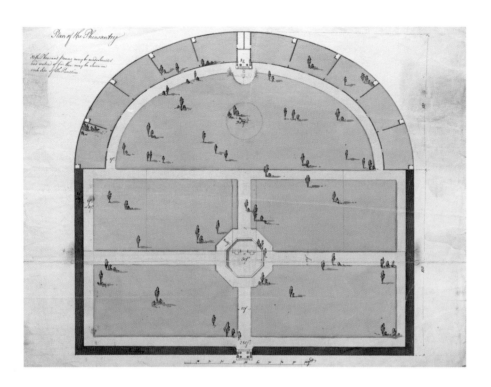

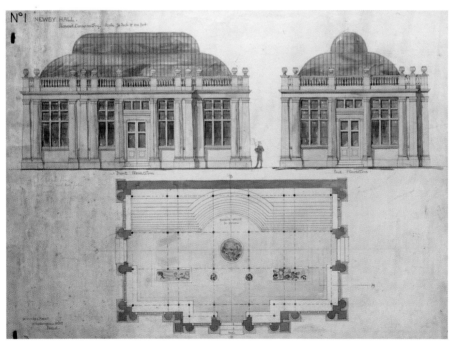

Figure 21
Plan of the Pheasantry,
Newby Park by William
Chambers, pen, ink
and coloured wash,
37.4 x 49.5cms (WYAS,
WYL5013/D/1/18/1)

Figure 22
Plan and elevations of
the Conservatory by
William Burges, pen,
ink and coloured wash,
50 x 66.3cms (WYAS,
WYL5013/D/1/22/1)

(later the R.I.B.A.), and rebuilt Wrest Park, his aunt's ancestral seat in Bedfordshire, to his own designs in the style of a French eighteenth century chateau.[26] As a young man living at Newby Hall, in addition to designing the new dining room and other facilities there, he also indulged in schemes for public buildings, including designs for an unidentified church and proposed alterations to the House of Correction in Ripon.[27] He may have been responsible for collecting a number of drawings of riding schools in London and elsewhere in 1823 possibly in connection with his own plans for such a building at Newby.[28]

Some of the drawings for unexecuted buildings are particularly striking and revealing. There are a plan and design by William Chambers for a pheasantry (figure 21), although it is not clear whether these were intended for Newby or Baldersby.[29] There are also schemes for proposed alterations at Gautby, the Vyner family house in Lincolnshire, by R.W.F. Brettingham and William Lindley in 1799–1803. Since the house was demolished in 1874, they provide essential clues as to how it may have looked.[30] Whilst working on the churches at Newby and Studley Royal in the 1870s, William Burges was also consulted about a conservatory at Newby (figure 22) and proposed estate cottages at Studley.[31] Neither project materialised.

Although this material has been separated from the main body of the estate archives for many years, it is important to see it in that context. For example, related items deposited in Leeds in the 1950s include a set of engraved plans of the grounds of the Spanish royal palace at Aranjuez in 1777.[32] They were presumably acquired by the 2nd Lord Grantham in the course of his tour of duty as ambassador there. There is also a large bundle of seventeenth and eighteenth century engraved maps and plans of French and Italian cities, particularly Turin, including views of churches and antiquities, which were most probably acquired in connection with his Grand Tour.[33] Oddments include some sketches of Jacobean houses such as Aston Hall and Charlecote in Warwickshire. They are watermarked 1837 and therefore may be taken to be the work of Earl de Grey.[34] There is a sectional drawing for the stairs to the satin dressing room at Newby dated 1806 and signed with Lord Grantham's monogram.[35] From an earlier period there are plans of the new manor house which

John Etty was to build for Sir William Robinson at Strensall in 1695[36] and plans of the King's Manor in York for proposed developments there 1726–1750. No doubt the latter arose from the interest as lessee of Sir Tancred Robinson, elder brother of the 1st Lord Grantham.[37] There is also a drawing for a dome, which Lindsay Boynton thinks may be attributed to Colen Campbell.[38] Among the records left by Sir Robert Vyner, the London goldsmith and banker who founded his family's fortunes, is an agreement about his house in Lombard Street in 1674, rebuilt after the Great Fire, which incorporates a plan showing its arrangement around a central courtyard with tenements fronting onto Lombard Street itself, Sherbourn Lane and Abchurch Lane. The site was destroyed by the construction of King William Street after 1829.[39]

Another element in this collection which needs to be viewed in conjunction with the main estate archive is a group of plans for the grounds and gardens. They include an anonymous early plan of c.1700 (figure 23), Thomas White's proposals of 1766

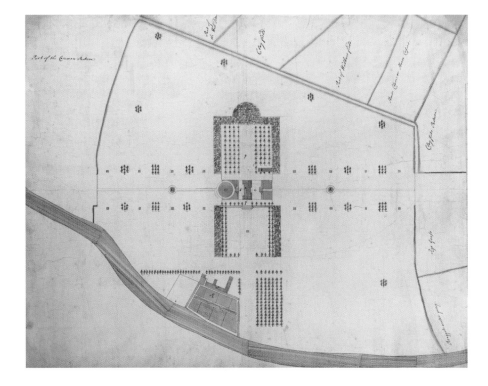

Figure 23
Plan of Newby Hall estate, anon, pen, ink and coloured wash, c.1700 (WYAS, WYL5013/D/1/1/1)

Figure 24
Photograph of the Entrance
to the Sculpture Gallery
on the south front, end
19th century, 17.7 x 21.7cms
(WYAS, WYL5013/D/1/22/11)

and William Burges' scheme for gates, terraces, the statue walk and the unexecuted conservatory also mentioned.[40] Comparison with the engraved view by Kip c.1720[41] suggests that the early proposals were mostly executed. It shows rectangular clumps of trees alternating with statues arranged in avenues east and west of the house, and formal gardens on the north and south sides. However, a feature missing from the Kip engraving is an avenue running south from the house to the river. The statues also appear to have been omitted from the final realisation. It is interesting, however, to compare these items with an early eighteenth century painting of the west front of the house, which hangs at Newby, and a garden design made by Peter Aram, the gardener there at this time, which has survived among the archives of the neighbouring Ripley Castle estate.[42] Was Aram the original designer or merely the executant? This formal scheme was replaced by Thomas White's informal parkland planting in the 1760s, although his plan still shows the arrangement of carriage drives serving the front door on the west side, soon to be transferred to the east front in Weddell's rearrangement. This remains the basis of the present landscape of the park and the Burges proposals were designed to sit within it. Alongside these garden plans is a small group of photographs of the house. They are mostly exterior views and although undated, were probably taken c.1870, before the stone gate piers to the entrance front were constructed. They show massive chimney stacks, since removed, on the projecting wings of the east front,[43] and a view of the library so heavily furnished that the details of Adam's decoration are largely obscured (figure 24).[44] This is the only interior view, but it fills a gap in our knowledge between John Buckler's sketches of 1816–1817 and the photographs taken for *Country Life* in 1937.[45]

This immensely rich collection of drawings must be one of the finest to come from any English country house. It illuminates the architectural ambitions of a web of inter-related families, but its kernel deals with the work undertaken for William Weddell, whose interests and activities have a constant memorial here.

Taste, Travel and the Reform of Culture in the 1760s

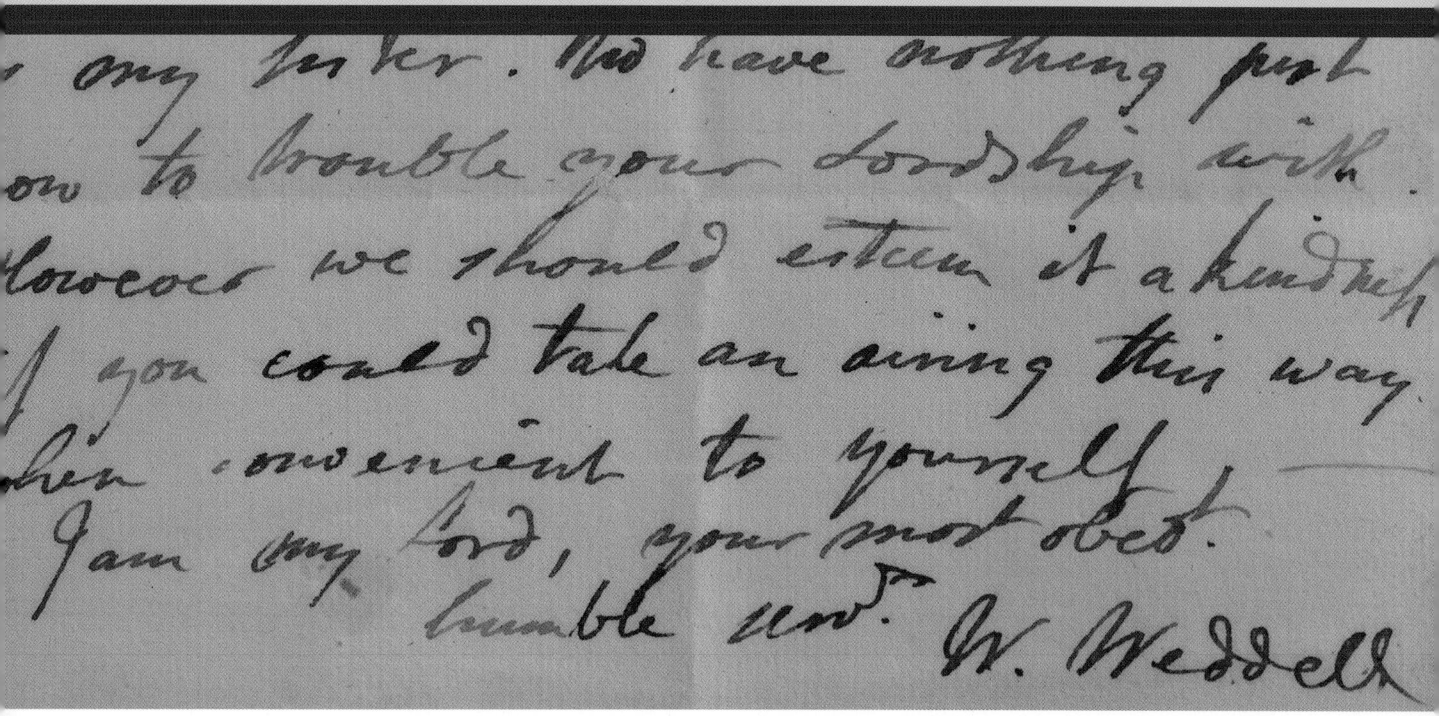
my sister. We have nothing just
now to trouble your Lordship with.
However we should esteem it a kindness
if you could take an airing this way
when convenient to yourself,
I am my Lord, your most obed.
humble servt. W. Weddell

A man who has not been in Italy, is always conscious of an inferiority, from his not having seen what it is expected a man should see. The grand object of travelling is to see the shores of the Mediterranean. On those shores were the four great Empires of the world: the Assyrian, the Persian, the Grecian, and the Roman. All our religion, almost all our law, almost all our arts, almost all that sets us above savages, have come to us from the shores of the Mediterranean.[1]

Figure 25
The Sculpture Gallery at Newby Hall with bust of William Weddell by Joseph Nollekens (courtesy of Newby Hall and Jerry Hardman-Jones)

Figure 26
Letter from William Weddell to Thomas Robinson, 17 August 1762 (WYAS, WYL150/6037(13731)

This familiar quote, from Dr. Johnson, serves to make vividly clear the extent to which the Grand Tour – the young gentleman's extended period of travel on the continent – was about both the supposedly timeless values of the classical heritage, and the immediate, intimate experience of individuals. As an historical phenomenon, the Grand Tour begs the question of how standards of taste and value are perceived and felt, how, in Dr. Johnson's terms, a sense of cultural 'inferiority' and, logically, 'superiority' is created and experienced subjectively. His comments show, too, that it was understood in this way not only by those who participated in it (the aristocracy and gentry, the writers, artists and architects, and increasingly, the aspirant middle-class) but those who did not.

With his intensive travels in the Low Countries and France in 1763–1764, and his similarly dedicated tour of Switzerland and Italy in 1764–1765, with his patronage of artists, designers and architects, and in his purchase of Old Master paintings and antiquities, Weddell can be viewed as the consummate Grand Tourist, educated in the classical cultures that formed mankind's 'grand object' and well-informed about the mores and manners of modern Europe. But we would be mistaken in thinking of him as simply archetypal, as if his activities and responses could be made to stand in for those of an entire class. Weddell's Grand Tour was, for a start, exceptionally productive. Quite simply there was more patronage, more buying, more doing and seeing than we encounter in many Tours of the period. Moreover, what he bought and the tastes these represent were, if not avant-garde in the sense we would understand the term, at the leading edge of contemporary taste in the 1760s.

In considering these points, we should remember that Weddell did not have the absolute social assurance that characterised many Grand Tourists in this era. Although well-educated and affiliated with the highest echelons of British society, he did not have a distinguished pedigree.[2] Most importantly of all, Weddell's Grand Tour came at a moment of rapid and momentous cultural change in Britain. The period 1763–1765 witnessed an immense flood of new tourists going to Europe, with the old values of the upper class both affirmed and disturbed.[3]

I want to consider the documented facets of Weddell's life during the period of his travels as elements in elite self-formation.[4] This is to heed Dian Kriz's advice that we must try to analyse 'the ongoing and often vexed processes of identity formation (both individual and communal) that are effected through the social exchanges, institutional forms, and representational practices' encompassed by the Grand Tour.[5] What is at stake, then, is the formation of what the influential social analyst Pierre Bourdieu terms the 'habitus', the clustered body of tastes and dispositions exhibited in an individual which marks his or her social status in relation to others, and which is predicated on but also contributes to a complex amassing of different kinds of capital (educational, social, cultural, as well as monetary). The habitus is how subjectivity, with all that implies about personal choice and emotional investment, functions socially, with all this suggests about shared values and distinctions of class and rank.[6]

What was at stake in the cultural economy of the Grand Tour was, at its most basic level, an exchange of money for cultural capital kept from being expressed as such under the language of 'virtu', as was acknowledged occasionally from within Weddell's circle.[7] The intention here is to consider Weddell's Grand Tour as an element in the formation of an historically specific habitus, one which is unique to Weddell in its totality, but whose different elements are shared with a number of overlapping groups, serving to associate him with specific social cohorts.

Occurring generally after formal education had ended and before marriage and a settled country life, the Grand Tour to Italy was intended as a moment of transformation or rite-of-passage, when the boy became a man. As Weddell's contemporary and associate Edward Gibbon put it, with a certain dry wit: 'According to the law of custom, and perhaps of reason, foreign travel compleats the education of an English gentleman.'[8] As Richard Lassels had indicated in his influential prefatory essay 'Concerning Travel' first published in his *Voyage to Italy* of 1670, 'Travelling preserves my young Nobleman from surfeiting of his Parents. . . It teacheth him wholesome hardness; to lie in beds that are none of his acquaintance.'[9] In practice, the Grand Tourist faced greater trials than hard beds: the seductive splendour of the Roman church, women, wine and the ruffians who preyed on travellers, overspending, corrupt art dealers, melancholy and disease were all widely discussed as hazards.

In the years of Weddell's travels, the utility of the Grand Tour was actively under interrogation. The traditions of criticising the aristocracy and the establishment had sharpened in the 1750s even before the Seven Years' War (1756–1763) brought such worries to a head with damning critiques of their luxury (most famously John Brown's *Estimate* of 1759).[10] The language of bluff masculine patriotism developed during mid-century among the political opposition moved into the mainstream and was used to attack the institution of aristocratic travel. A particularly vivid and pertinent example is the dialogue between 'Shaftesbury' and 'Locke' imagined by

Richard Hurd in his *Dialogues on the Uses of Foreign Travel* (1764). Here the ideas of 'hardiness' and 'hardening' from the old Grand Tour literature are revised and given an original social orientation. Hurd's 'Shaftesbury' puts the case for travel by caricaturing the young gentleman who has had only formal education but who has not seen the world:

To put the case at the best, suppose him to have been well whipped thro' one of our public schools, and to come full fraught, at length, with Latin and Greek, from his college. You see him, now, on the verge of the world, and just ready to step into it. But, good heavens, with what Principles and Manners! His spirit broken by the servile awe of pedants, and his body unfashioned by the genteeler exercises! Timid at the same time, and rude; illiberal, and ungraceful! . . . But now, on the other hand, let a young gentleman, who has been trained abroad; who has been accustomed to the sight and conversation of men; who has learnt his exercises, has some use of the languages, and has read his Horace or Homer in good company; Let such a one, at his return, make his appearance in the best societies; and see with what ease, and address, he sustains his part in them! how liberal his air and manner! how managed and decorous his delivery of himself!

Hurd is setting 'Shaftesbury' up here, for this line of argument gives 'Locke' the chance to complain that access to superior social rank is a matter only of superficial manners, of courtliness. Instead, 'Locke' proposes: 'What a reasonable man wants to know, is, The proper method of building up *men*: whereas your Lordship seems solicitous for little more than tricking out a set of fine Gentlemen.'[11] Hurd here succeeds in opening up a potential faultline within elite ideals of masculinity, between gentility as a socially desirable quality and an appropriate and necessary assistance to the political management of the modern British state, and gentility as a corrupting influence that undid manhood.

We face certain challenges when it comes to documenting Weddell's travels. For his first, aborted Tour, which took him through the Netherlands and through France to Paris where he stayed until February 1764, we have his own, in some ways perfunctory, diary.[12] But his second tour of 1764–1765, there is no diary. What we do have by way of compensation is a rich and revealing body of documentation relating to Thomas Robinson's slightly earlier Grand Tour in 1759–1761 and his trip to France in 1763. A kinsman, contemporary, and immediate neighbour (living at Newby Park), Robinson (1738–1786) exerted a significant influence on Weddell in these years. We can assume that he would have advised Weddell on his Tour, as would be usual when among such close friends, and even if we cannot take Robinson's words as Weddell's, they suggest the values and desires that surrounded the Grand Tour at this point.

At his bluffest, Robinson can appear as the kind of English bigot all too familiar to our European neighbours today. In Turin at the beginning of his Tour in August 1759, he wrote to his brother complaining about the effete gentlemen of the Continent:

I am sure to meet several very pretty young Counts and Marquis, with bags & swords, but I always think when I see them how easily you would lick them, & that tho' they should draw their swords, that a knock on the mark would lay these tough Fellows flat. Any but you would think that tough meant hardy & stout, but tell them to look tough out in the Westminster Dictionary, & they will find the meaning of it to be Proud, self-sufficient & conceited of themselves.[13]

This may be a boorish joke made in a personal letter, but it registers a sense of what was at stake in defining the English gentleman at this point. Its sentiments should not be forgotten even as we move into the ostensibly more rarefied realm of taste.

Travelling with his friends John Mytton, Thomas Wynn and James Grant, Robinson went to Milan, Florence and Naples, and then settled in Rome for the spring and summer of 1760. From here he conscientiously expressed the conventional sense of being almost entirely overwhelmed by a city where 'every Private House from the Stable yard to the Cabinet contains some Curiosity or other'.[14] As Chloe Chard has traced, such remarks reflect the widely-perceived danger that Rome could overwhelm, diminishing rather than enhancing a sense of selfhood.[15] But a few months later, in March 1760, Robinson has learnt enough to be able to reflect more carefully about the way culture is consumed there, and suggests in an intriguing way a sense that he has gained mastery over the city:

The Antiquities of Rome are one may say of several Sorts, some have been & are no more, of others there are Remains, either collected in the places where they stood from the first, or dispersed in Churches Palaces &c Erudition & Historical facts stamp a Merit upon some of them, & others owe to their Intrinsick Grandeur or Elegance. To each of these persons of different Turns will as their inclinations point them out, attach themselves. Some Persons will be satisfied with the base Idea that the Temple of Jupiter Capitolinus stood on the same hill as they themselves do, & I have seen others contemplate the remaining Columns of that Edifice without the least Attention to their former situation & the Difference with which People look upon these things except such as are really great of Beautiful, I imagine depends very greatly on the persons themselves. For I believe that in three days time a man may make himself enthusiastick or indifferent to these kinds of things. Now surely if one can tho' it be only by ye help of the Imagination create to one-self a new pleasure every day, who would not rather suffer himself to fancy he is pleased, than with too much grave good Sense exclude willingly a pleasure because an imaginary one. A Man therefore who has a Degree of Taste sufficient to relish the Works of Arts & a competent knowledge of facts that he can call forth & recollect when he pleases, had better for his own Satisfaction & Pleasure give way to a kind of Enthusiasm which many sensible People much to rigidly censure & condemn.

With a certain degree of warmth then I would advise any body to set out on such a Tour as that of ye Roman Antiquities, & he cannot but be pleased at the voluntary Delusion.[16]

Robinson presents Rome as an exemplary site of cultural distinction, where by passing judgment, the judger himself is judged and classified – as superficial or profound, superior or inferior. The threat to a sense of selfhood associated with being overwhelmed by the historical richness of the city has been not so much overcome, but mastered, in the sense that the threat can be appreciated pleasurably, the 'voluntary Delusion' which would usually be considered anathema to the well-educated, well-brought-up, upperclass man, can be indulged as a means of marking a superior taste in a fashion not easily reducible to rules.[17]

Robinson was careful to articulate a sense of how he possessed 'a Degree of Taste' in other fields as well. He gave a highly articulate account of his reservations about the refined style of Pietro da Cortona and Carlo Maratta, artists whose 'affected Contour & excess of Gracefulness made incorrectness less perceivable' thus corrupting taste until 'they have spoilt more painters than almost any thing can reform'.[18] And it was from his last weeks in Rome that Robinson penned the important letter detailing his views on the respective merits of Mengs and Batoni, pitching the 'Force' and 'Dignity' of the former against the affectedness, finicky detail and deceitful affectation of the latter. Comparing their treatments of the same theme from Homer, Robinson remarked: 'Menx has drawn Hector Andromache & Astyanax within the Walls of Troy, while Battoni's is il Signor Ettore, la Signora Andromache, & ill famicello Asyanaz on the Theatre in the Haymarket.'[19] Such judgements of taste rest on a terminology

and approach which contrasts the noble, truthful and British (or at least Anglo-Saxon) with the effete, deceitful and foreign, a set of oppositions reproduced throughout social and cultural criticism of these years.

We find the same themes of taste, judgement and patriotic sense repeated in the letters that were written when Robinson went back to the Continent in 1764, this time to stay in Paris. Here his bluff Englishness was contrasted to the despicable 'frivoleté' of the French, a characteristic that may be forgiven only as relieving the gloomier aspect of 'good English Common Sense'. And this sense of national pride was extended, tellingly, to contemporary taste, with Robinson's ambivalent view of the *goût grec* that then raged in Paris. Of the French, Robinson wrote that while 'their Taste is very much improved & in all Matters of Ornament they now almost entirely adopt the Antique' this rage for classicism was to be viewed sceptically, as 'Their Notions of Erudition on that head seem to be confined to calling everything a la Grecque.'[20] So even if fashionable Paris led the way in the revival of classical forms and motifs in the arts, they remained essentially frivolous and superficial compared to Britain's. In this, Robinson manifests the complex attitude towards

France which dominated in British culture. As a French satirist of the time had an English Grand Tourist say: 'We love France, and we hate the French.'[21] But it also, more specifically, chimes with the views of leading French artistic reformers and *philosophes*, for whom the *goût grec*, while preferable to the florid decorations of previous years, still needed to be more disciplined and refined and made more vigorous.[22] This, in turn, indicates the growing momentum behind cultural reform, on the Continent as well as in Britain, a movement for change registered linguistically in the notion of 'improvement', a term which was certainly applied to Weddell.[23]

Weddell's own Tour began when he sailed from Harwich on the 20 August 1763. Although his inheriting Newby Hall in 1762 was certainly a prompt, his Tour was part of a wave of travel after the Peace of Paris in February 1763. While tourism continued through the years of war (Robinson's tour was undertaken, after all, in the midst of the conflict) the peace treaty opened the floodgates, with a whole generation taking the opportunity to visit Paris and to travel on to Italy.[24]

Weddell was somewhat unusual in touring Holland first, though this was the third most popular Grand Tour destination after France and Italy. Weddell's diary of his tour suggests a dutiful, exhaustive and surely exhausting tour from town to town.[25] Yet if the diary provides little in the way of personal insight, it is telling nonetheless, in showing a serious, dedicated young traveller intent on seeing everything he can, learning and improving, developing 'a Degree of Taste'.

Sadly, the diary runs out of steam once Weddell reached Paris on the 24 September. Acclaimed as 'the Center of the Arts of Politeness, of Gallantry, and of good Company' by David Hume, 'the Centre of Taste, Magnificence, Beauty & every Thing that is polite' by William Cole, or, in the blunter words of Sterne, 'this city of seductions', we have little evidence for what precisely he did during the four months he spent there.[26] There could hardly be a better time for a wealthy Englishman to be in the French capital. As Edward Gibbon wrote during his time in Paris in March 1763: 'The name of Englishman inspires as great an idea at Paris as that of a Roman could at Carthage, after the defeat of Hannibal. Indeed, the French are almost excessive.

Figure 28
Gobelins tapestry, medallion
from *Les Armours des Dieux*
(courtesy of Newby Hall
and Jerry Hardman-Jones)

From being very unjustly esteemed a set of pirates and Barbarians, we are now, by a more agreeable injustice, looked upon as a nation of Philosophers and Patriots.'[27] In the wake of Britain's victory over France, in a war that had done profound damage to the French economy, the English were looked to as heroes, perhaps, but also, as potentially lucrative customers. This was certainly the case for the Gobelins manufactory. Officially the King's tapestry works, foreign customers were being actively sought in these tough times, and it was understood by this point that 'if any Stranger chuses to buy any of the Works, it is very easy to have leave'.[28] Specifically, an innovative new design on a medallion format had been developed by Boucher with an eye on the English market. The first set of the medallion tapestries *Les Amours des Dieux*, had been bought in the summer of 1763 by an Englishman, George William, Lord Coventry. Weddell was to be the second customer, probably on this trip to Paris, when we know from his diary he visited the collection of Jean de Julienne, a director of the Gobelins.[29] They were to be followed by four more English clients, all purchasing a set of the same design. As Smollett was to note:

The tapestry of the Gobelins is brought to an amazing degree of perfection; and I am surprised that this furniture is not more in fashion among the great, who alone are able to purchase it. It would be a most elegant and magnificent ornament, which would always nobly distinguish their apartments from those of an inferior rank; and in this they would run no risque of being rivalled by the bourgeois.[30]

Understood in this way, Weddell's purchase of the Gobelins tapestry (figure 28) could serve in a very immediate way to distinguish him from the 'bourgeois' (or, more pointedly, his own bourgeois heritage) and line him up with the most distinguished and fashionable members of the nobility, or at least those able to afford the most extravagantly expensive of luxury goods.[31]

With his sister's health in a perilous state, Weddell was eventually persuaded to return to England after four months in Paris, arriving back in February 1764.[32] He was able to set off again, however, in August 1764 in the company of a friend from Cambridge, the Rev. William Palgrave (c.1735–1799).[33] They reached Switzerland together at the beginning of September, staying there for most of that month and seeking out, without success, Jean-Jacques Rousseau. They then travelled to Chambray, Turin, Milan and Florence, where they had dinner with the British representative, Horace Mann at the beginning of December. They reached Rome on Christmas Eve 1764.[34] Here they remained, apart from a three-week trip to Naples in March, until June 1765, returning to England in July of that year.[35]

This was an extended stay in Rome. We should assume that he took a tour of antiquities early in his stay, apparently conducted by the Abbé Peter Grant, a Scots Jesuit and a senior figure in the expatriate community.[36] Most vital was the recommendation of Weddell to the dominant English art dealer Thomas Jenkins, furnished by Robinson.[37] It was Jenkins who supplied Weddell with enough antiquities to fill twelve cases, which he exported along with eighty-six paintings in the spring of 1765. Weddell also commissioned contemporary art, most importantly two paintings from Gavin Hamilton, then only recently established as the leading

British painter in Rome, their subjects drawn from Milton but represented in the classical idiom of Guido Reni. With these purchases, Weddell compounded his association with artistic reform. An archaeologist and art dealer as well as a painter (and a gentleman – he came from a landed background) Hamilton was considered as a leading artistic reformer, casting aside the pettiness and prettiness which prevailed in favour of a severe dedication to classical values. He could, indeed, count that archetypal artistic reformer Winckelmann among his fans.[38] The seventeenth century Bolognese style deployed in the paintings he produced for Weddell reinforced the idea of his art having a reforming function: Reni, along with the Caracci, were cast as artistic reformers who had rescued art from its decline in the later sixteenth century by drawing together all the characteristics of ideal art, characteristics increasingly diffused through artistic specialisation.[39]

Alongside this extensive consumer activity, Weddell found time to sit for his portrait. Like Robinson before him he was shown in company (in this case with Palgrave and

his servant Christopher I'Anson) in a conversation piece by the English painter Nathaniel Dance (figure 30), and he was also painted by Batoni in a full-length and on a smaller format (the careful choice Robinson had made between him and Mengs was not available now, as Mengs had been in Spain since 1761).[40] The performed nature of the Grand Tour, the acts of judgement and taste which were so heavily invested with significance, are resolved through portraiture into informal gestures which speak powerfully of a form of socially-exclusive male intimacy.[41] The conversation-piece format, with its modest scale and apparent lack of pretension, was an ideal medium for communicating the convivial nature of Grand Tourism, and the ease with which a highly-invested social role (being a man of taste) could be inhabited.

A different kind of informality reigns even in the grandiose full-length by Batoni, where Weddell gestures back to the highly esteemed ancient sculpture known

Figure 30
Portrait of William Weddell, Rev. William Palgrave and Christopher I'Anson, by Nathaniel Dance, oil on canvas, 1765, 97 x 134cms (National Trust Photographic Library/Michael Cooper)

as the Ariadne (also known as the dying Cleopatra) in the Museo Pio-Clementino.[42] The Ariadne had already featured, in the form of a table-top reduction, in Batoni's portrait of Charles John Crowle, and in his portrait of Thomas Dundas, where the relatively flamboyant gesture of the sitter suggests a more ostentatious presentation than is evident in the Weddell portrait. Batoni was to use it as a device at least three times more, twice for English sitters and once for a Polish Count.[43] Weddell's portrait thus joins him to an elite, both because he is painted by Batoni and because he is shown at ease with a canonical classical work, thus registering his social performance through the most elegantly simple, modest of gestures. As a commentator remarked of the painting when it was seen at Newby Hall in 1802, Weddell was shown as 'contemplating the statue of a dying Cleopatra; a subject that points out his Classical turn, at the same time that his countenance marks a mind peculiarly adapted to the pursuit of every thing connected with elegance and taste, arts and letters'.[44]

The lack of detailed or personal documentation about Weddell's Tour means that we are left to speculate about its significance. But with Robinson's experience in mind, we can see that the sheer extent of his activity is in itself telling, speaking of a degree of 'Enthusiasm' which offered a response to the criticism of the Grand Tour as a mere luxury and which operated as a way of measuring and marking different degrees of 'Taste' and value. Further dimensions of Weddell's Grand Tour experience may be revealed in his membership of the Roman Club, 'A weekly convivial meeting' for ex-Grand Tourists established by Edward Gibbon in London in 1766. The membership of this 'Roman Club' was identified by a surviving member in the mid-nineteenth century, John Holroyd, Earl of Sheffield (1735–1821), and this allows us to identify a group of men tightly unified in their cultural, educational and social capital as well as by their experience of the Grand Tour.[45] All but one were born between 1735 and 1746; more than half were university-educated, in an era when only a third of the English upper class went to university; and all undertook their Tour in the early 1760s, mainly in 1764–1765, when they were in their mid-twenties. Rather than being simply typical of Grand Tourists, they were unusually highly-educated, and tended towards relative maturity, presumably reflecting the general obstacle to travel presented by the recent war.[46] The majority also had notable military associations, having served either in the regular army or in the militia, including Weddell.[47] Given that Britain had just come out of a vast, bloody and protracted conflict, this might not be surprising. For decades the militia had been viewed with suspicion, for its associations with Jacobite opposition. But the exigency of the Seven Years' War, and ideological shifts in the last years of George II's reign and around the accession of George III in 1760, resuscitated ideals of martial masculinity. For Weddell and his peers, taking up arms as a member of the militia was not just about service to the nation, as we might understand it; it was also, in more specifically eighteenth century terms, about living out a classical ideal of citizenship, reviving in the modern context and at a personal level the masculine virtues of the ancients.[48]

By way of Weddell's association with Gibbon's Roman Club, we may begin to give some definition to the psychological and social dimensions of Weddell's Tour. Gibbon cast his membership of the Roman Club as a response to the profound need he felt for self-possession, driven by his experience of the militia and of travel abroad shared, quite completely, with Weddell: 'in the militia I was armed with power; in my travels, I was exempt from controul: and as I approached, as I gradually passed my thirtieth year, I began to feel the desire of being master in my own house'.[49] Given the furious round of 'improvement' at Newby Hall which followed Weddell's Grand Tour, these are suggestive words indeed.

Weddell's Newby Hall and Gibbon's *Decline and Fall of the Roman Empire* are comparable monuments to the Grand Tour experience of the 1760s and the pressures towards cultural reform that emerged in these years. The evidence is that the kinds of cultural disposition formed in such men were fragile, and short-lived. There is clear evidence that among the other members of the Roman Club, the conviviality and robust high-living that prevailed could lead to more disreputable and damaging behaviour.[50] More generally, the political and cultural consensus that prevailed in the early 1760s soon fell apart, and questions of taste and aesthetic value became politically charged in an especially divisive way.[51] Weddell had relied on Jenkins as a source of antiquities, and these were always heavily 'restored' by Cavaceppi and

Figure 31
The Barberini Venus (detail)
(courtesy of Newby Hall)

Nollekens.[52] Such restorative practices came under increasing fire in the 1760s and 1770s, as more exacting standards of connoisseurial judgement and historical authenticity came into play.[53] In a slightly different way, we may speculate about the mystery that surrounded how much Weddell paid for the renowned Venus (figure 31). Was this grand purchase in danger of appearing in bad taste, particularly as criticism of the aristocratic Grand Tour and the luxurious tastes of the upper class escalated? Certainly, an early commentator reported that it was 'said to have been bought at so high a price as induced Mr Weddell to conceal from his friends the enormous expence in which this indulgence of his favourite propensity involved him'.[54] And it may be telling that the highly refined Adam taste exemplified at Newby Hall was not repeated in the later decoration of Weddell's London house.[55] Charles Townley was to complain to Jenkins that 'It's a Pity Mr Weddell should have been induced to overcharge his Gallery with Ornaments, but the Adams I am told have done it every where.'[56]

William Weddell's Grand Tour and the subsequent transformation of Newby Hall offers an enlightening episode in the history of elite taste in England; they show him to be an innovative patron, engaged with the most advanced tastes of his time, tastes whose value was in part based on the potential they had for becoming quickly outmoded, as was made apparent in the contemporary ambivalence around the *goût grec*. Weddell's Grand Tour also offers a revealing case study of the means by which such tastes were constituted, how they functioned socially and, ultimately, how they belonged to and would always be passing into, history.

William Weddell and his Architects

Celia Fiennes' description of Newby Hall in 1697 as 'the finest house I saw in Yorkshire' is confirmed by the view of the west front (now the garden front) drawn by Leonard Knyff and published in *Britannia Illustrata* in 1707 (figure 32).[1] The three storey, nine bay house, with a flat balustraded roof and belvedere from which to view the great formal gardens laid out by London and Wise, represented the culmination of approximately fifteen years of improvements undertaken by an unknown architect for Sir Edward Blackett, 2nd Bt., who had bought the house in 1677. Further improvements (though unrecorded) are likely to have been made by Sir Edward's sons, Sir Edward Blackett, 3rd Bt., Captain R.N. (d.1756) and John Blackett of Newby, before 1748 when the property was sold to Richard Elcock for £9,530 (figure 33).[2]

The purchase of Newby fulfilled the terms of a formal contract made by Thomas Weddell of Earswick, Yorkshire, in January 1714 on the occasion of the marriage of his nephew, Richard Elcock, to his niece, Barbara Tomlinson, settling on them

Figure 32
View of Newby Hall from *Britannia Illustrata* (1707–26) by Johannes Kip and Leonard Knyff, engraving (WYAS, WYL5013/D/1/1/4a)

Figure 33
View of East Front of Newby Hall (courtesy of Newby Hall)

and their male issue £10,000 'to be laid out in the purchase of lands'.[3] As 'no such purchase of land' had been made by July 1747 when Thomas Weddell died, and as the Elcock's two sons, Thomas (b.1734) and William (b.1736), were still under age, it was imperative that Richard Elcock – who was required by his uncle to take the name of Weddell – spend his legacy as soon as possible.

In June 1748, a few months after purchasing Newby from the Blacketts, Richard Elcock Weddell paid Daniel Garret's bill for £12 1s, a sum roughly the cost of designs for a new or rebuilt house. It cannot be mere coincidence that Garret (d.1753) was then in the throes of reconstructing Wallington Hall, Northumberland, for Sir Walter Calverley Blackett, a cousin by marriage of the Newby Blacketts. There is, however, no physical sign of work by Garret at Newby, and Richard Weddell does not seem to have contemplated major alterations before 1755 – the year his eldest son Thomas came of age – when he turned to John Carr, who was well on the way to becoming Yorkshire's leading architect.[4] Though the precise date of Carr's arrival on the scene remains uncertain, we do know that improvements were in progress by 1757 when Richard Weddell's cousin, the Hon. Thomas Robinson (later 2nd Baron Grantham) of Newby (now Baldersby) Park, visited Newby Hall and described it as 'still a staring red & white house'.[5]

The earliest known drawing by Carr for Newby is an undated plan showing the H-shaped house as existing after 1758, with two symmetrical pavilions with Venetian windows on the east front, separated from the main block by 'Little Court[s]' (figure 34).[6] These pavilions evolved from the late seventeenth century outbuildings depicted by Knyff at the back of the house, and were to be further developed in the late 1760s and early 1770s by William Weddell.

Carr's proposed alterations to the main body of the house – distinguished by grey wash – were to move the principal entrance from the west to the east front; to create a large apsidal drawing-room on the west front; and to add semi-circular bows to the corner projections on this side. The revised entrance was the only part of his scheme that was implemented (figure 33); but exactly when this work was begun and just

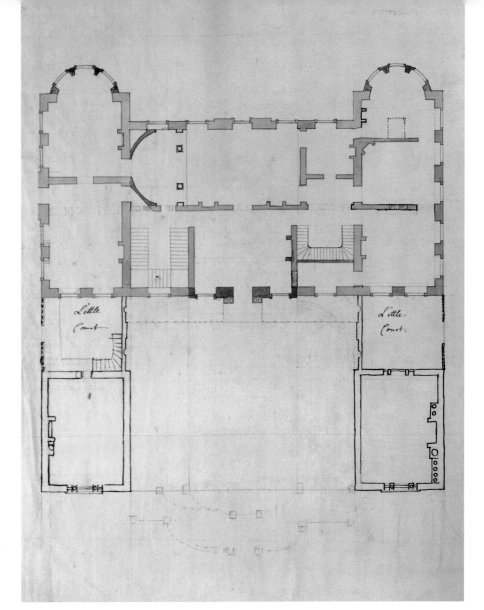

Figure 34
Early plan for alterations
to ground floor by John Carr,
pen, ink and coloured
wash, mid-18th century,
38.5 x 54.5cms (WYAS,
WYL5013/D/1/3/2)

how far it had progressed at the time of Richard Weddell's death in December 1762
is not known.

The architectural future of Newby was now in the hands of the twenty-one-year-old
William Weddell. Having satisfactorily settled certain legal matters regarding his
inheritance,[7] William set off for Paris which became a Mecca for English travellers
as soon as the treaty ending the Seven Years' War was signed in February 1763.
What he saw and did there remains a matter for speculation. The current rage for
the *goût grec* was inescapable, and a visit to the royal Gobelins factory is more than
likely. There he would have been shown coloured drawings of an apartment lined
with the firm's new Boucher-Neilson medallion tapestries which he ordered for his
drawing-room on his next visit.[8]

He returned to England in February 1764 to attend to his ailing sister, Margaret, a spinster, and to make a new will.[9] Six months later he set off again, this time for Italy accompanied by his friend, Reverend William Palgrave, and his servant, l'Anson. His cousin, Thomas Robinson, who knew Italy well having spent three years there from 1759 to 1761, provided him with letters of introduction, and the poet, Thomas Grey, recommended things for him to see.

The purchases and acquaintances Weddell made in Rome are dealt with in depth by Ruth Guilding and Martin Myrone and need not be repeated here. Suffice to say that the nineteen chests full of statues and other works of art, which he sent back from Italy in March, April and May 1765, had a formative effect on the building history of Newby. Whether any work had been done there in his absence is unclear.[10]

Improvements to the house started immediately upon Weddell's return in August 1765, and were in full swing by 23 September when Thomas Robinson saw 'workmen of all sorts' there. 'We approve of the Alterations', he wrote; but, apart from the removal of the roof-top belvedere, he did not specify what they were.[11] Weddell's first requirement was to provide a suitable home for his large collection of marbles; the most expedient solution was to join the existing service pavilions to the house and make the whole of the south wing into a gallery.

Fortunately, he had no need to search for an architect as he was already committed to Carr. He also had ideas of his own, which he was able to draw, albeit crudely, and plenty of advice from Thomas Robinson, who seems to have inherited some talent as an amateur architect from his maternal grandfather, Thomas Worsley of Hovingham.

The shell of the gallery, designed and executed by Carr in 1765, was a fairly simple single storey brick building finished with stone balustrades and quoins to harmonise with the main body of the house, a two storey centrepiece with a Tuscan porch on the south or garden front, and a canted bow on the east end. For the interior Carr planned a conventional arrangement of three sections divided by columnar screens, which evidently did not satisfy Weddell's desire for an evocative antique setting for his antique marbles.

Advice was sought from Sir William Chambers, Thomas Robinson's architect at Newby (now Baldersby) Park in 1766. Chambers's extemporaneous suggestions (figure 35) – hastily noted on a copy of Carr's plan – were that the central space should be 'fitted up rather plain and arched' so as to distinguish it from the smaller, flat ceiled spaces on either side; that the three windows in the bow be blocked so as to form a semi-circular apse for 'Venus Life' (also known as the Jenkins' Venus); and that the large sarcophagus be placed opposite the entrance. Only the apse was executed.

Figure 35
Elevation and ground plan of the Sculpture Gallery by John Carr with suggestions by William Chambers, pen and ink, before 1764, 43 x 32.5cms (WYAS, WYL5013/D/1/6/2)

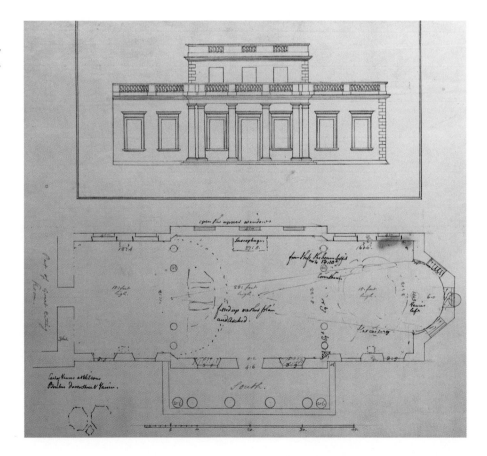

Figure 36
Plan and laid-out wall
elevations of the Entrance
Hall by Robert Adam,
pen, ink and grey wash,
87 x 62.5cms (WYAS,
WYL5013/D/1/8/1)

Weddell also seems to have called upon James 'Athenian' Stuart who had been working since c.1755 at Wentworth Woodhouse for his great friend and political patron, the Marquis of Rockingham. Though there is no evidence of Stuart's participation in the gallery, he is known to have been acquainted with Weddell by 1767 and was almost certainly responsible for the architectural organ case in the hall.[12] This is shown in outline as a pre-existing object in Adam's 'Design for finishing the four sides of the Hall' which was presumably made in 1769 at the same time as his ceiling design (figure 36).[13]

There was nothing unusual about Weddell showing Carr's designs to other architects for comment. Edwin Lascelles showed Carr's Palladian designs for Harewood to Adam

Figure 37
Section of the end wall of
the Sculpture Gallery next
to the Dining Room by Robert
Adam, pen, ink and wash,
46.5 x 62cms (WYAS,
WYL5013/D/1/6/13)

in June 1758, which he proceeded to 'tickle. . . up'; Sir Nathaniel Curzon asked for Adam's opinion on Matthew Brettingham's designs for Kedleston, to which he 'proposed alterations' and, to flatter Curzon, told him to 'call them his own fancies'.[14] What is remarkable about the Carr drawing annotated by Chambers is its survival.

The kudos of being returned to Parliament as member for Hull, and being elected to the Society of Dilettanti in March and April 1766 respectively had the effect of raising Weddell's self-esteem as well as his expectations for Newby. Entering into the swim of things must have made him realise, if he had not done so earlier, how hopelessly old fashioned and out of touch with the current neo-classical taste his house was. If there was anyone who could imbue the dull and static sculpture gallery built by Carr with the novelty, variety and grandeur of ancient Rome, it was Robert Adam, whose inventive genius in remodelling the interiors of existing buildings in an original 'antique' style had been brought to bear on two great Yorkshire houses: Harewood and Nostell, where he supplanted Carr in 1765 and James Paine in August 1766. Adam's arrival at Newby coincided almost exactly with his intervention at Nostell.

His initial plan was a perfectly symmetrical one, with a central domed rotunda and four niches, flanked by two smaller square rooms, each with a large apse at the end and niches on the remaining walls (figure 37). George Dance's prize-winning design of 1763 for *A Public Gallery for Statues, Pictures, etc.* provided him with an appropriate model. Although his boldly articulated scheme satisfied Weddell's demand for individual settings for his major pieces, it was completely at odds with the existing room into which it opened. Clearly, the gallery could not be treated in isolation.[15] It had to be related to the rest of the house; or, rather, the rest of the house had to be re-planned in relation to it. And so it was by 1767.[16]

The circuit round the reception rooms went counter clockwise from the hall to the drawing-room on the west front – for which Weddell had already ordered a set of Boucher-Neilson medallion tapestries on a mauve-pink ground – and from there into an apsidal ante-room with enriched stucco pilasters and panels of painted grisailles

on pale purple grounds. This small but 'singularly beautiful, chaste and classical' room,[17] sadly destroyed in the early nineteenth century, was a prelude to the visually exciting sequence of the large dining-room with screened apses at either end (converted to the present library by the 3rd Lord Grantham in 1807) followed by the gallery.

The long vista from the west end of the dining-room through the door in the apse at the opposite end into the 'penetralia of the temple – the museum, or gallery of statues'[18] is one of Adam's most successful achievements in picturesque planning (figure 38). Weddell must have been delighted to see the stiff, inelegant spaces of his sculpture gallery emerge with the diversified contours of an antique Roman interior and to gain a suite of fashionable neo-classical reception rooms in the process.

His private apartment on the north side of the house, consisting of a dressing-room (now the boudoir), a parlour, and study (now the drawing-room), was fairly straightforward by comparison, and, apart from the study created in 1769, did not require Adam's attention. Nothing of any consequence was done on the first floor until after the design of the staircase was agreed in 1771.[19] Instead of proceeding with the grand imperial stair in Adam's initial plan, Weddell decided for reasons of economy to keep the old stair and have Adam bring it up to date with new wrought-iron balusters like those at Osterley, carved strings, and an oval rose-and-star boss on the ceiling.[20]

A screen of Ionic columns of green Cippolino marble was erected on the ground floor in accordance with Adam's 1766–1767 plan, but what, if anything, was planned at that date for the first floor landing is not known. The earliest surviving drawing of the entire staircase is the 'Section. . .' made by William Belwood, the carpenter/joiner in charge of its execution (figure 39).[21] This has been mistakenly identified as a design by Belwood, as have other drawings in his hand. It is, in fact, a copy or record drawing of a design by Adam which has not survived. Instead of perpetuating this

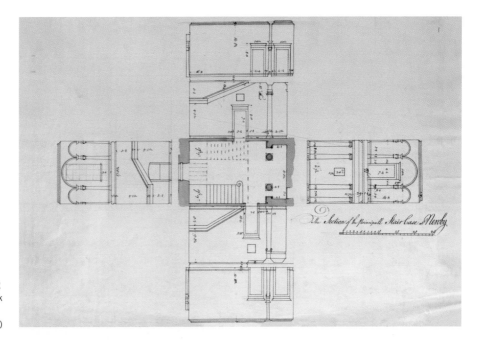

Figure 39
Laid-out wall elevations of staircase and upper landing by William Belwood, pen, ink and grey wash 38 x 54cms (WYAS, WYL5013/D/1/12/1)

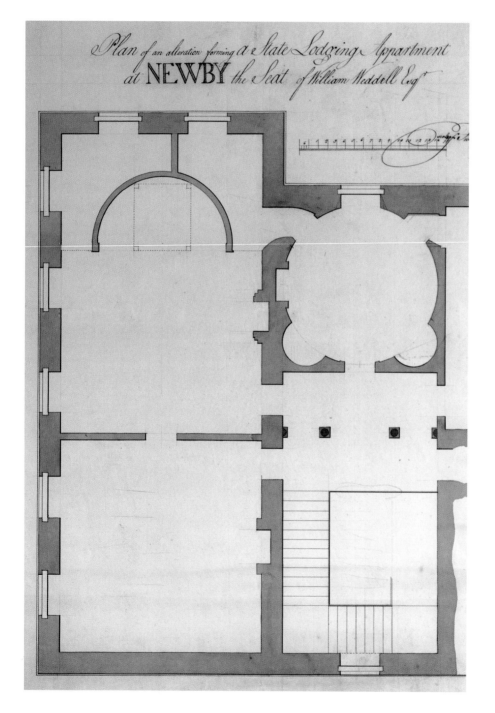

Plan of an alteration forming a State Lodging Appartment at NEWBY the Seat of William Weddell Esq.

Figure 40
Plan of alterations to form
a State Lodging Apartment
(over dining and anti-rooms)
by Robert Adam (previously
attributed to Belwood), pen, ink
and grey wash 43.8 x 31cms
(WYAS, WYL5013/D/1/14/1)

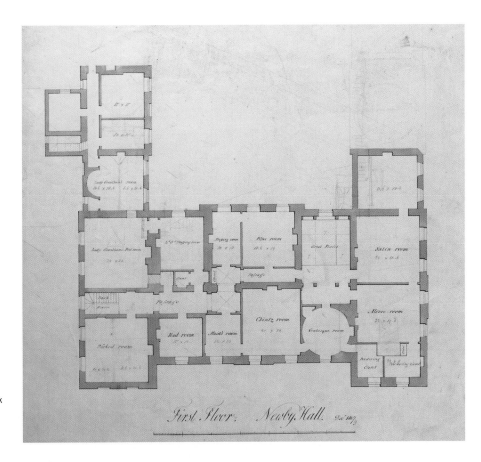

Figure 41

Plan of the first floor by Thomas Robinson, pen, ink and grey wash, 1807, 51.5 x 55.8cms (WYAS, WYL5013/D/1/3/5)

error, as I did in *The Genius of Robert Adam His Interiors*,[22] I should have realised that a professional architect of Adam's calibre would never have left the completion of a space as important as the main staircase to the trusted joiner who was supervising the execution of his work.

Belwood has also been wrongly credited with the 'State Lodging Appartment' behind the arcaded screen at the top of the stairs (figure 40).[23] The fluid plan of this suite, consisting of a circular dressing-room, a large 'Alcove Room' and square bedroom occupying the space above the ante-room and dining-room, is absolutely typical of Adam and comparable to his plan of 1772 for the *piano nobile* of Weddell's town house in Upper Brook Street, Grosvenor Square.[24]

Adam's designs for the state bedroom apartment and the principal bedroom adjacent to it (also mistakenly attributed to Belwood[25]) were probably made in 1771, the same year as his designs for the staircase hall. 1771 was a special year for Weddell; in February he married Elizabeth Ramsden, sister of Sir John Ramsden, 4th Bt. of Byram in Yorkshire, and half-sister of Lady Rockingham, wife of his close friend at Wentworth Woodhouse. The date of their marriage is recorded on one of the trophies on the hall ceiling designed in 1769.[26]

Among the drawings in the Newby Hall Archives is a plan of the first floor, drawn in 1807 by Thomas Robinson, the 3rd Baron Grantham (later Earl de Grey), who inherited Newby Hall after Weddell's death in 1792, showing the state bedroom apartment as executed with modifications (figure 41).[27] The circular dressing-room, for example, was executed without the large apses in Adam's plan, and was subsequently decorated with four arched panels of grotesque ornament painted by Elizabeth Weddell.[28] If Mrs. Weddell had any assistance here, it would have been from Adam, not Belwood. Her 'grotesques' are of approximately the same date, 1775, as Adam's Etruscan-style decorations in the dressing-room at Osterley. She was also responsible for painting the walls of the parlour in the farmhouse at Newby with ornaments derived from a plate in Piranesi's *L'Antichità Romane*.[29] 1776 has been suggested as the date of these decorations.[30]

William Belwood of York (1739–1790) was brought to Newby by Adam in 1766 or 1767 to supervise the execution of his interiors as he had been doing at Harewood since 1765. Having also worked at Syon in 1763–1765, Belwood understood what Adam wanted, and could be relied upon to undertake the construction of the dome and several apses and niches in the gallery and dining-room to his satisfaction. In addition, he was a competent, though uninspired, draughtsman, capable of copying out plans and making large-scale working drawings from Adam's designs, as well as technical diagrams of timber framing.[31] Having such drawings made on site instead of in the London office helped to hasten the completion of the project and reduce the costs, which must have pleased Weddell greatly. Their survival in the Newby Hall Archives is both remarkable and instructive; they are worthy of further research.

Figure 42
Elevation of the East Front of Stable Block by William Belwood, pen, ink and coloured wash, 26 x 36.5cms (WYAS, WYL5013/D/1/20/3)

By 1774 Belwood had sufficient experience in executing Adam's designs to establish himself as an independent architectural designer in York. He continued working at Newby until his death in 1790 on equal ground with Adam rather than as a subordinate. His principal works at Newby Hall are as follows: the stable block designed in 1777 (figure 42), which has in the past been credited to Adam, though he, unlike John Carr, is not known to have submitted designs;[32] the Chambersian entrance porch of c.1777, chosen by Weddell in preference to the more classical, costly and comprehensive scheme submitted by Adam in November 1776, which introduced a large pediment over the three central bays and proposed rendering the entire brick front to look like stone (figure 43), an idea that may have come from Weddell as it also appears in Belwood's design;[33] and, also of 1777, the main entrance lodges in a heavy Palladian style, with large 'antique' cinerary urns on the gate piers, copied from examples in Weddell's collection.[34]

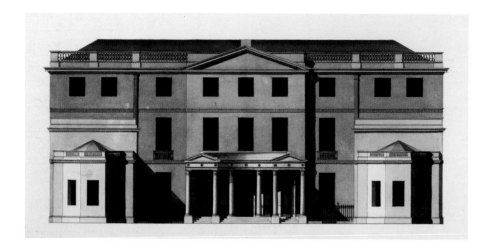

Figure 43
Elevation of the East Front
(entrance porch) by Robert
Adam, pen, ink and grey wash,
45 x 61cms (WYAS,
WYL5013/D/1/3/8)

An additional storey containing the Weddell's private apartment was added by Belwood to the north wing in 1784.[35] Though it included an alcove dressing-room inspired by Adam's state bedroom apartment in the south wing, its plan has none of the diversity and movement of the latter; the two apartments cannot possibly have been designed by the same person. Building a symmetrical storey above the domed sculpture gallery was very much more difficult. Belwood unadvisedly added a further room to Adam's state bedroom apartment above the small room at the west end of the gallery in 1784, which later proved troublesome.[36]

One of Belwood's last jobs at Newby Hall in 1789 was to provide new bookcases for the study or library, a square room in the north west corner, which had been finished by Adam approximately twenty years earlier. His three bookcases (one large and two small) with scrolled pediments and acanthus corbels may be identified with the three bookcases listed in the 1792 inventory of the contents of the library.[37] Their design is totally different from the four architectural bookcases in an uncompromising neo-classical style with Tuscan pilasters, full pediments and acroteria included in Adam's laid-out wall elevations of 1769 (figure 44).[38] We have no documentary evidence that Adam's bookcases were executed, nor do we know of any alternative library furniture prior to Belwood's. Because Belwood's cases were executed, it has been assumed that Adam's were not;[39] but this may not be true.

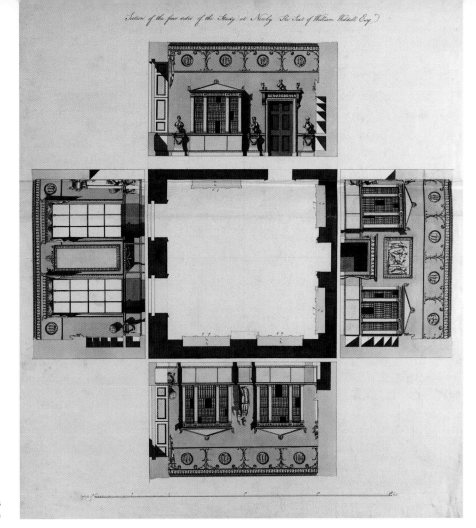

Section of the four sides of the Study at Newby The Seat of William Weddell Esq.)

Figure 44
Plan and laid-out wall
elevations of the Library by
Robert Adam, pen, ink and
coloured wash, 72 x 54cms
(WYAS, WYL5013/D/1/10/1)

The most likely reason for commissioning bookcase designs in 1789 was Weddell's need for greater book capacity, which could easily have been achieved by adding a central section to Adam's two bookcases on the west wall were it not for their classical pediments. The most expedient and economic solution was to remove the pediments and replace them by Belwood's elastic scrolled and semi-circular tops. We therefore have Belwood building upon Adam.

In the words of Lady Grantham, wife of Thomas Robinson, Weddell's cousin, who employed Belwood at Newby (now Baldersby) Park in 1782: 'Mr. Belwood. . . seems a very civil intelligent man and is not too great to execute other people's schemes'.[40]

The Sculpture Gallery
at Newby Hall

William Weddell was born a commoner, his future status dependent upon entry into political life and ownership of land. When a lucky inheritance gave him both he acted judiciously: his Grand Tour and subsequent cultural pursuits, his club memberships, political alliances and his marriage, brought him the attributes of a typical member of the landed Whig majority in Yorkshire. In this context, his acquisition of a notable collection of antique sculpture, and a superlatively decorated gallery to house it, seem inevitable, rather than surprising (figure 46).

Figure 45
The Barberini Venus, marble, 162cms (courtesy of Christie's Images Ltd)

Figure 46
The Sculpture Gallery at Newby Hall (courtesy of Newby Hall and Jerry Hardman-Jones)

With the exception of the architectural drawings for Newby, Weddell's papers reveal little about his motivations for collecting sculpture, instead being almost entirely orientated on politics and his role in the service of his party and of his mentor, the 2nd Marquis of Rockingham. But at the time collecting antique sculpture was understood as a moral activity that ennobled the collector, and which could lend prestige and public legitimacy to the newly rich, with fortunes amassed in trade or commerce.[1] In this light, Weddell's newly acquired cultural tastes provided the appropriate backdrop to his public, political activity and a source of continuing status and private solace when public life eventually failed him. Significantly, the epitaph chosen for his tomb gave greater prominence to Weddell's works of 'taste' (a quality concomitant with moral virtue), than to any of the other achievements of his lifetime.

Weddell came into his inheritance in 1762 at the age of 26. His family had only recently made the leap into the gentry class after a bachelor great-uncle left money to his father, Richard Elcock, conditional on his taking his family name of Weddell and on making acquisitions of land, which included the Newby estate.[2] Having already spent a period in the militia, at Grey's Inn and at St. John's College Cambridge,[3] William Weddell now set out to redress the balance of his education and experience by making the Grand Tour. This experience would 'form his taste' giving him the ability to offer opinions on questions of beauty and its nature, the necessary qualification to take part in cultural discourse in the mid-eighteenth century.[4] His sister's illness forced him to return home almost at once,[5] but in August of 1764 he re-embarked on his travels, taking with him a contemporary of student days, his friend the Reverend Mr. William Palgrave.

Weddell had already attached himself to his neighbour and future political patron the 2nd Marquis of Rockingham, Prime Minister in 1762, and a serious connoisseur of medals, bronzes and marble antiquities (an alliance strengthened in 1771 by his marriage to Lady Rockingham's half-sister, Elizabeth Ramsden). Fired by social emulation, his carefully planned Grand Tour seems to have been undertaken in the spirit of a buying trip to furnish his newly improved house in a manner appropriate to his standing in the county. Advice was taken and contacts with the most prominent dealers were arranged in advance, so that Weddell was able to fill and send back some nineteen packing crates of antiquities,[6] as Palgrave described, writing from Italy to James Grant of Castle Grant, who had provided some letters of introduction:

Your letters to Jenkins and Hamilton were not in vain, for Weddell is buying such a quantity of pictures, marbles etc. as will astonish the West Riding of Yorkshire. . .[7]

Figure 47
The Barberini Venus (detail), marble (courtesy of Newby Hall)

Weddell and Palgrave had dined with Horace Mann when they passed through Florence in December 1764,[8] and Mann gave them his customary introduction to Cardinal Albani,[9] but as the pair spoke little French and no Italian they perhaps lacked the finesse to exploit these occasions.[10] Help was also provided by Weddell's cousin, Thomas Robinson, the 2nd Lord Grantham, who had travelled to Rome in 1760–1761, who now supplied letters of introduction to the antiquities dealer Thomas Jenkins in Rome, where the pair spent the winter and spring of 1765. Jenkins replied with letters of thanks enclosing gifts,[11] informing Robinson that Weddell had purchased 'the greatest part of the Paintings and Sculpture that I had'.[12] Weddell had apparently gone immediately to Jenkins and spent the bulk of his money there, his picture collection being acquired at considerably less expense during the last weeks of his tour.[13] He also visited Piranesi's museum-cum-showroom in the Palazzo Tommati and purchased a cauldron and a made-up pedestal.[14]

In February of 1767, when a letter from Thomas Jenkins (dated 31 December 1766, one of a series itemising antiquities recently excavated in Rome) was read before the Society of Antiquaries, another collector Lyde Browne explained that five of the prestigious pieces described were 'all in the possession of Mr. Weddell, Member of Parliament for Hull'.[15] The overheated antiquities market had been squeezed by tighter export regulations, the difficulties of large-scale excavation, and the papacy's rights to make compulsory purchases of the best pieces, so that Weddell's collection acquired, *en bloc*, from Jenkins comprised a more miscellaneous ensemble than those formed earlier in the century. Lyde Browne listed a bust of Minerva, colossal heads of Hercules and a female deity, a statue of Brutus,[16] and a 'Pavonazzo urn[17],' about which Jenkins wrote:

. . .a little distance from the Porta Latina in a Vineyard near the Road of that Name, in the month of May 1765 – were discovered a number of Sepulcral Urns, or Sarcophagus's, many of which had the remains of Bodies in them; some are of Plain Marble, others ornamented with Basso relievos, of various Stiles of Sculpture, and of different times; supposed to have been placed where found in the lower Ages, when it was customary to take Sarcophagus and Urns of Marble already made, even even from Baths and other Sepulchers, and adopt them for their own use – amongst those urns was one of an uncommon size and Beauty being of Pavonazza and is presumed to be the most Elegant Munument of its kind hitherto discovered.[18]

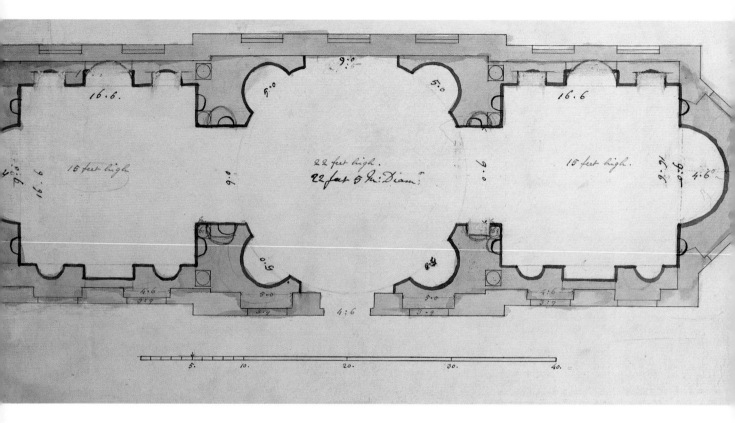

Jenkins capitalised on his membership of the Society of Antiquaries to publicise and authenticate his merchandise, but kept silent on the subject of Weddell's most expensive acquisition. Accounts of how the celebrated 'Barberini Venus' (figures 45 and 47) was acquired and restored by Jenkins differ wildly,[19] but all the commentators agree that Weddell paid a high price for it and was duped by Jenkins into believing it to be a complete and perfect example of the type made famous in the Medici Venus, although its head and numerous other details had been restored, probably by Cavaceppi.[20] Most authorities agree that the headless statue was recovered by Gavin Hamilton in the cellars of the Barberini Palace, and after passing through the hands of more than one restorer it was brought onto the market as an unrestored piece by Jenkins in 1764. This statue, which Winckelmann called the 'Jenkins Venus',[21] became one of the most famous antiquities in any English collection of

Figure 48
Ground plan of the Sculpture Gallery with sketch overlaid by Robert Adam, pen, ink and grey wash, 18 x 42cms (WYAS, WYL5013/D/1/6/4)

the period, an object of continuing admiration and curiosity. Eighteenth century commentators had produced a mass of adulatory writings on the Medici Venus, some discerning an insidious quality in her smile, and a dangerous sensuality in her fleshy beauty, which might be capable of overwhelming aesthetic appreciation and unmanning the spectator. To redress this balance, at Newby a statue of Minerva stood in an adjacent niche, creating an opposition between Virtue and Pleasure personified which would have been understood by the visitors and viewers who were familiar with Joseph Spence's *Polymetis* (1747).[22] The ideal beauty of the Newby Venus and the consummate skill of Bartolomeo Cavaceppi, her restorer-cum-fabricator, were reaffirmed in 2002 when the Venus was sold at Christie's Fine Art Auctioneers in London to a private collection overseas, fetching the sum of nearly £8 million.[23]

Just as he had gone to the foremost dealer in Rome for his sculpture, so in 1766[24] (the year in which he was proposed for membership of the Society of Dilettanti and returned to Parliament as the member for Hull), Weddell gave the commission for the gallery and attendant works at Newby to the most fashionable architect in Britain, Robert Adam,[25] the shell of the gallery having already been completed by John Carr.[26] Later in his life, Weddell enjoyed a reputation as an amateur designer and arbiter of taste amongst his friends,[27] and he may have already begun to plan the arrangement of his marbles in Carr's half-finished shell as soon as they were uncrated, for a sketch-plan of the gallery of c.1765 annotated by Sir William Chambers[28] places the great sarcophagus in the central room, and the Venus at the end of the long vista. When Adam came to the project, the gallery and adjoining dining room (now converted for use as a library) were the first, most urgent works to which he addressed himself,[29] and a sketch of c.1766–1767 (figure 48) shows his own design for the gallery overlaid upon the existing space,[30] which resembled a conventional long gallery. Adam's presentation drawings for the Newby gallery are undated, but one of the two designs for the coloured floor pavement is dated 1772, and the whole ensemble was apparently nearing completion by 1778.[31] William Belwood, a local builder, executed the work, and among working drawings in his hand at West Yorkshire Archive Service is one for a pedestal with ram mask, sphinx and patera decorations,[32] several of which were executed in wood and gesso.

Figure 49
View of the interior of
the Sculpture Gallery
(courtesy of Newby Hall
and Jerry Hardman-Jones)

Adam transformed the plan of the Newby gallery into an interlinking sequence of two rectangular rooms flanking a central, circular one (figure 49), all enlivened by apses, niches and recesses of various sizes, drawing upon the popular formulas of the French Academy architectural competitions,[33] and perhaps on his design for a library for Lansdowne House of c.1766, with two domes flanking a central rectangle. The decorative methods which he had previously followed so effectively, transposing the classical motifs which he had studied in Rome directly onto the architecture of rooms such as the Saloon at Kedleston,[34] were outdated, and inappropriate for the much smaller scale of the buildings at Newby. The formula which he adopted for Newby was instead anticipated in the small gallery or 'Casino' built in 1764 behind the Adam brothers' house in Grosvenor Street, as a setting to display marbles and casts bought by James Adam from Rome to visiting clients[35]. (figure 50) The complex decorative treatment of the walls, with niches framed by panels and pilasters with rainceau patterns and grotesque work, acted as a foil for the sculpture, the richness of the 'pseudo-archaeological'[36] decoration perhaps owing a debt to the influence of Piranesi, and more directly, to Robert Adam's apprenticeship to Charles-Louis Clerisseau, his drawing master in Rome during the 1750s. The Newby gallery's low-relief decoration in the Adam brothers' newly patented stucco[37] and ornamental tondos with painted grisailles, has its origins in designs after the Antique made during the 1750s: Clerisseau's sketch, *Maison Antique*, (Hermitage)[38] and Adam's *Reconstruction based on the Roman Bath* (figure 52)[39] present a sequence of multi-faceted architectonic spaces, smothered with three-dimensional decoration. Clerisseau's designs eventually culminated in the 'antique house' which he began to design for Catherine the Great in 1773; this had a grand plan featuring a number

Figure 51
Section of frieze of the Vitruvian scroll mid-way between the dado and cornice in the Sculpture Gallery (courtesy of Newby Hall and David Winpenny)

Figure 52
Reconstruction based on the Roman baths by Robert Adam, pen and wash, c.1750, 27.6 x 40cm (courtesy of the Trustees of the Sir John Soane's Museum – Adam Drawings 56, 45)

of tripartite room sequences, one of which mirrors the Newby gallery, and included several highly decorated rooms for the display of sculpture.[40]

The gallery at Newby was tiny, but its three-part shape offered numerous surfaces which could be articulated by means of surface decoration, contrasting curves and flattened areas against which to place free-standing sculpture. A frieze of Vitruvian scroll mid-way between dado and cornice links all three rooms and subdivides the walls into three bands (figure 51). The main wall colour was a 'pale strawberry ground'.[41] The two end rooms, where the more miscellaneous pieces in the collection are displayed, have thickly ornamented ceilings, and walls set with stucco reliefs of scenes from the story of Bacchus and Ariadne. The decoration of the walls of the central, domed space is more chaste but the heads of the niches containing the most significant full-length statues in the collection have rich stuccoed decoration highly reminiscent of the type of Renaissance decoration found in the loggia of the

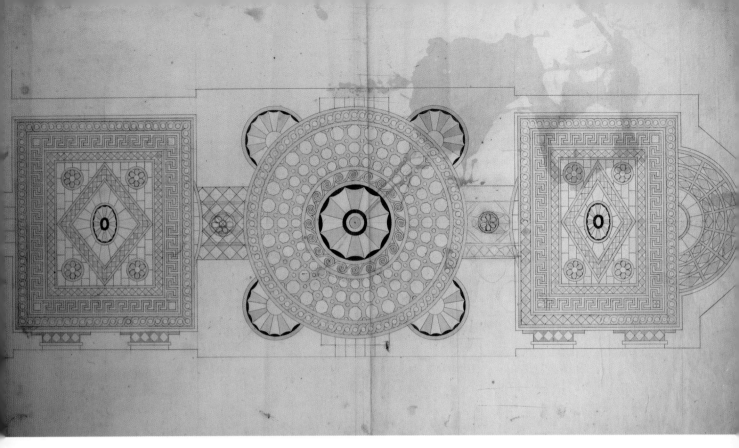

Villa Madama, which Adam had studied closely.[42] Adam's two (unexecuted) designs for a polychrome pavement (figure 53) would have further contributed to the overall linkage of gallery surfaces by colour and design in the manner of Roman Renaissance architecture,[43] throwing the white marble of the sculptures into contrast. The ensemble represented a sophisticated application of polychrome design to the basic tripartite space already devised by Carr, and a successful synthesis of other design sources from Adam's personal repertory, which relied upon the strong application of ornament and symmetrical balance to unify its parts.

Weddell himself was eager to show off his collection to friends and country house visitors; Lord Rockingham saw and commented on the collection, apparently then in situ, in 1774,[44] the same year in which Townley had sent Jenkins his first account of it. However, it was the dealer Thomas Jenkins boast that he had guided and informed Weddell's taste completely,[45] and he intended to benefit from any publicity surrounding them, sending frequent enquiries about it to Townley,[46] and directing his other customers, such as Mr. Barry, there, 'as he will there see how well things look when properly placed.'[47] Jenkins was already urging Townley to visit Newby in 1768, when the marbles were temporarily arranged in Carr's half-finished gallery,[48] and through his efforts the statues of Venus and Minerva became even more celebrated: in 1768 he arranged for a cast of the Minerva to be made for the Empress of Russia

Figure 53
Scaled drawing, design for pavement by Robert Adam, pen, ink and coloured wash with pencil, 67.5 x 110cms (WYAS, WYL5013/D/1/6/23)

Figure 54
Alabaster urn on a neo-classical pedestal designed by Robert Adam (courtesy of Newby Hall and Jerry Hardman-Jones)

through the agency of 'General Schwoloff, the Moscovit',[49] and two years later Townley received his own cast.[50] The Venus was the gallery's showpiece: in 1779 Robert Darley, Lord Grantham's former secretary, wrote to his employer, 'We rode over in the morning to see Mr. Weddell's Venus',[51] and Lord and Lady Rockingham even pressed Mrs. Weddell in an attempt to discover its cost, 'but Mrs. Weddell pleaded ignorance'.[52] Weddell was reputed to have given a lump sum in payment of anything from £1,500 to £6,000,[53] and to have made further annual payments until his death in 1792, but both buyer and seller kept the terms of the transaction a secret.[54] The sensation caused by the statue must have satisfied Weddell that he had made the right decision in this. After Weddell's death his steward Christopher l'Anson, who had accompanied him to Italy as his personal servant, testified that he had spent the colossal sum of more than £8,000 on sculpture.[55]

Weddell's gallery aimed at the character of a private museum, such as the famous and elaborately embellished Villa Albani in Rome. According to the latest fashions in display in the new galleries of the Museo Pio Clementino, the small sarcophagi in the farthest room were furnished with wooden covers and placed upon monopodia brackets, to be used as pedestals for other pieces, and a few of the foremost figure sculptures in the collection were also given antique pedestals, or pedestals made up from antique fragments. The rest stood on neo-classical pedestals of painted wood designed by Adam and executed by the builder William Belwood (some of which disguised heating devices). On the same axis as the gallery, with sight lines leading towards the Pavonazza bath at its far end, the dining room was also designed with five niches for sculpture in its apsidal ends,[56] which were instead filled with large alabaster urns designed by Adam, containing candles (figure 54). In 1802 a visitor commented that the light from these vases assisted 'the magic effect with which the mind is impressed when we look through the door at the. . . penetralia of the Temple'. Weddell's dinner guests would have moved between the two rooms admiring the statues by candlelight following the contemporary vogue for such practices described by Goethe, the flickering glow and contrasting light and shade giving the marbles the appearance, almost, of animated flesh.[57]

The gallery's decoration was sufficiently 'antiquarian' in character to content Weddell and his friends, but within a decade of its conception it was considered spurious and incorrect, when held up to the exacting scholarly standards of Charles Townley. Weddell did visit the house-museum that Townley was constructing in Park Street in the late 1770s,[58] with its archaeologically sourced cornices and columbarium niches,[59] but only when the gallery at Newby was all but complete. The difference in the two men's approach to their collections was immense: Townley made acquisitions based upon his constantly developing understanding of taxonomy and methodology,[60] and with the exception of his entrance hall, the rooms in his house were sparingly decorated, the better to show off his sculpture collection. Weddell chose his gallery as he did his collection, by going to the most highly recommended supplier; he displayed genuine antiquities alongside 'modern' or neo-classical pieces,[61] and his collection was 'complete', according to Jenkins,[62] once sufficient pieces of the right size and style had been amassed to fill the spaces allocated to them. In Townley's view, the Newby gallery was 'overcharged' with ornaments;[63] the Adam brothers' taste was an anathema to him, and he had recently concluded a legal dispute with them over their unsolicited proposal to adapt one of the newly finished houses in their Portland Place development for his occupation.[64] By contrast, the design for a new sculpture gallery at Towneley Hall which Townley commissioned from Joseph Bonomi in c.1783 was comparably ornate and richly decorated with grotesquerie,[65] but this decoration was based more precisely on surviving antique examples, in keeping with Townley's more rigorous scholarship.

The sculpture collection at Newby was recorded in the probate inventory made on Weddell's death,[66] but Townley's plan made in 1779 provides the only record of its arrangement during his lifetime (figure 55)[67], when the great marble bath was placed at the end of the vista in the third room, and the statue of Venus was in a niche in the central rotunda where it remained until 2002.[68] Townley's plan also reveals that the sculpture was more sparsely arranged in 1779, perhaps because some of the pieces there now were then placed elsewhere in the house, and only brought into the gallery under the terms of the probate inventory of 1794.[69] The whole concept of the Newby gallery was dependent on symmetry, and Adam had designed

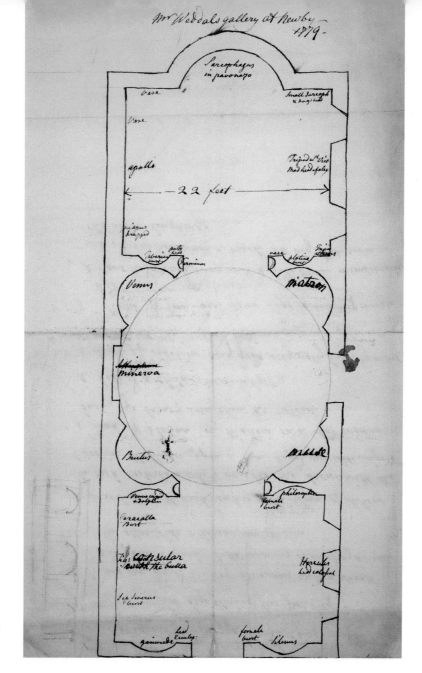

Figure 55
Plan of the Sculpture
Gallery at Newby Hall by
Charles Townley, pen and
ink, 1779, 37.5 x 22.7cms
(© The British Museum,
BM/TP/15/1/1)

niches and pedestals tailored to many of the larger pieces, anchoring them in one
position for perpetuity. Pieces were grouped in pairs, or with smaller pieces, busts
or urns flanking a larger one, standing against the curved and projecting walls of the
gallery. In 1779, Weddell was still apparently anxious to improve the harmony and
symmetry of the room by acquiring a few more well-matched pieces, as Jenkins wrote
to Townley:

Mr. Weddell will of course have been to visit you, as this gentleman wants a few things to
complete his excellent collection, I took the liberty of mentioning to him that he might see
with you sketches of my urns and sphinx etc; what a fine object for him my cupid would be,
and I think he still wants one or two figures of that size.[70]

Figure 56
Antique sculpture of an Ibis
at Newby Hall, marble,
70cms (courtesy of Newby
Hall and David Winpenny)

Weddell's antique sculpture of an Ibis (figure 56) stood upon the tripod with a cauldron bought from Piranesi.[71] Animal pieces such as the Ibis were still comparatively rare in English collections (although some at Castle Howard were acquired in the early eighteenth century),[72] becoming more common from the 1770s as part of a category of new types of work replacing the large statues which were now more expensive and difficult to obtain.[73] Also among the smaller pieces in the collection were two triangular pedestals or tripod bases, one decorated with Bacchic figures in low relief, the other with Victories, both of which were illustrated in Volume III of Bartolomeo Cavaceppi's *Raccolta d'antiche Statue*. These had been in private collections in Rome for at least two centuries before this, having been recorded in both the Codex Coburgensis of the mid-sixteenth century and the Dal Pozzo-Albani albums (now in the Royal Library Windsor).[74]

Figure 57
Terminal sculpture of Eros,
marble, 134cms (courtesy
of Newby Hall and David
Winpenny)

Another superlative piece, Weddell's terminal figure of Eros (figure 57) was first described by Winckelmann in 1763 as an unrestored torso with one wing stump, in the possession of an Englishman living in Rome.[75] Jenkins had publicised this piece, newly excavated at Hadrian's Villa, in a letter to the Society of Antiquaries dated 30 March 1763:

A Terminus of the first rate sculpture, and still more singular on account of its Subject: the proportions are a mixture of Masculino and Feminino, with the parts of generation of the former, it has wings like a Cupid or Genius. with the Skin of a Goat thrown over part of the Body – as it wants the head it is Difficult to Ascertain with prescision what it represented: it was first believed to have been an Hermaphrodite, which skin of a Goat does not prevent, as that in the Florentine gallery has such a skin lying by it 'alluding probably to the Forest in Which the Union happened'. neither would the wings be foreign to the Subject, as they might be supposed to imply that Love was the cause of this Union – this opinion of this

Antiquity – but on its being seen by a Gentleman of great learning and Judgement, he so finds still more upon it and supposes it to have represented the four Elements – Terminus signifying the Earth. the Wings the Air. the Mixture of Sexes the Harmony of the Soul. to strengthen which he would have placed in the Head the wings of a Butterfly. by the Soul the Ancients meant Fire. it being often used to represent the Soul; and he further proposes to put in one hand a Vase which would signify water, by this means would be explain'd, Fire, Water, Air and Earth: how far this explanation may merit approbation I know not – in the meantime if any more probable conjectures occurr to any Gentleman of the Society the honour of his Opinion will be received as a most Particular favour.[76]

Mistaken for a hermaphrodite or female figure by Winckelmann,[77] it was restored by Cavaceppi to conform with his theory as a *'Genio Femminile'*, and illustrated in his *Raccolte* Volume I in 1768, where it was by now described as belonging to Weddell.

Did William Weddell appreciate the historical value of his collection, or was his sculpture gallery, as Stephen Bann has suggested, simply the ahistorical 'realisation of an ideal vision, where history as process plays no part?'[78] Probably, as long as they were celebrated, he was comparatively indifferent to the discussions over his sculptures at the Society of Antiquaries. For him, rather, connoisseurship was demonstrably bound up with politics and status, both at the meetings of the Rockingham Club in London where the noblemen and gentlemen supporters of his party met (ostensibly) to discuss literature and antiquities,[79] and at the 'Roman Club', a weekly convivial meeting of which Gibbon was also a founder member. Superficially, Weddell's aspirational version of connoisseurship owed much to his patron Lord Rockingham, an aristocratic virtuoso whose judgements Weddell plainly valued. His rather condescending and pointed appraisal of the gallery was appended to one of the many political screeds, which Weddell received from him,

I was most exceedingly pleased with all I saw at Newby. Several of the antique marbles are really good, Great part of the Venus fine – I like also much of the tall Minerva and the little head of Minerva is very sweet and pleasing. The visit there and the disagreeable conjuncture of probable events in this country etc. made me revive a wish to once more revisit Italy.[80]

Perhaps Rockingham feared that Weddell prized his sculptures more for their beauty and fame than for the proper virtue which they were supposed to inspire; that they had, in fact, become an end in themselves. Rockingham advocated an

ideal of Augustan 'retreat' in the country and the civilising pursuits which could be followed there, as the counterbalance to metropolitan and political life.[81] His secretary and amanuensis, Edmund Burke (the individual responsible for defining the 'works of the imagination and the elegant arts' as occupying a higher plane than other works of taste, by their power to stimulate the pleasures of the imagination),[82] was also, by no coincidence, a collector of antique sculpture.[83] By contrast, Weddell's connoisseurship marked a weakening of the link between taste and public virtue endorsed earlier in the century by commentators such as Lord Shaftesbury, 'a tentative valorisation of the aesthetic for its own sake.'[84] Through the improvement and presentation of his house with its paintings and sculptures, his lands and political seat, Weddell signalled his desire to 'belong'. In private, with his old travelling companion William Palgrave, he could indulge fully in his pleasurable fantasy of a life in Arcadian retreat, conducted according to the norms of the classical past, with Palgrave obligingly comparing his gardens to 'Pan's parlour', and Mrs. Weddell 'like another Aspasia' presiding over the breakfast table laid out in the portico of the Newby Sculpture gallery.[85]

In public life, however, Weddell's role was never more than that of satellite in Rockingham's court: having secured his patronage and entered Parliament in 1766, he behaved as a reliable, if reticent backbencher, supporting his policies, but apparently never speaking in the house.[86] His fortunes fell with his patron's when the King's support was lost, and the Whigs entered a long period in opposition; Rockingham's death in 1782, and Weddell's failure to win the seat of York two years later brought to an end any hopes that he may have held of a seat in the House of Lords.[87] In 1788 he was feeling 'almost a disgust about every manoeuvre

Figure 59
Monument to William
Weddell at Ripon Cathedral
(courtesy of Ripon Cathedral
and David Winpenny)

in the political world',[88] his moderate political beliefs leaving him increasingly isolated among the Foxite Whigs. Edmund Burke felt a similar pessimism, and addressed a long epistle (intended for public circulation) to Weddell in 1792, lamenting the betrayal of his party's 'ancient values',[89] those values which had originally led its members to image themselves as 'Romans'.

Weddell died in 1792. Both in public and private, antique models had provided the frame in which his reputation was made. His whole life can be seen as a struggle to be confirmed by his peers and betters as a 'man of taste', and the significance of his gallery, presented as a site for moral instruction and learning which was also a place of consummate style, costliness, entertainment and sensation, lay in its power to underpin that identification. His monument, erected by his widow in Ripon Cathedral, was a fusion of classical elements drawn from the repertoire which he had favoured (figure 59): Weddell's bust by Nollekens[90] stood upon a copy of his antique pedestal purchased from Piranesi, the whole enclosed beneath a small-scale copy of the Lanthorne of Demosthenes taken from Stuart and Revett's *Antiquities of Athens*, which Weddell had recently used as the model for a greenhouse.[91] By comparison with the three-storey mausoleum commemorating Rockingham at Wentworth,[92] a structure of solid, Palladian forms erected in 1785–1791, it is a minor production, but (like the Newby gallery) its bravura neo-classical design was carefully selected as another mark of Weddell's exemplary 'taste'. This prized attribute was singled out for commemoration above any other achievement, both in the inscription on his monument, and in another contemporary memorial:

To the Memory of William Weddell Esq: of Newby,
In whom every Virtue that Enobles the Mind was United with every Elegance that Adorns it, this Monument, a faint Emblem of his Refined Taste, is dedicated by his Widow. . .[93]

In all the works of Art and Genius No Man ever possessed a more correct Judgement, or a more distinguishing Taste. . .[94]

Notes

West Yorkshire Archive Service

The Newby Hall drawings and other historical documents are archived at West Yorkshire Archive Service (WYAS), Chapeltown Road, Sheepscar, Leeds LS7 3AP. Tel 0113 214 5814. References to the drawings in the West Yorkshire Archives have the following prefix: WYL5013/D. The former reference prefix for this collection was NH.

William Weddell – a biographical note
Kerry Bristol and Jill Low

1 The standard sources on William Weddell and Newby Hall are John Cornforth, 'Newby Hall, North Yorkshire I–III,' *Country Life*, 7, 14 and 21, June 1979, pp. 1802–1806, 1918–1921, and 2006–2009; Jill Low, 'The Art and Architectural Patronage of William Weddell (1736–1792) of Newby Hall and His Circle', unpublished PhD thesis, University of Leeds, 1981; and Eileen Harris, *The Genius of Robert Adam His Interiors*, London and New Haven, 2001, pp. 212–231. I am grateful to Dr. Low for allowing me to edit and amend parts of her thesis for this essay. Staff at the West Yorkshire Archive Service (Leeds) and Sheffield Archives have been helpful at very short notice and I would like to thank them for their assistance.

2 On this point, see Richard Wilson and Alan Mackley, *Creating Paradise. The Building of the English Country House 1660–1880*, London and New York, 2000, pp. 11–46.

3 Information on these early members of the Weddell family can be found in the Skaife Manuscripts at York City Archives and M. J. Sayer, 'William Weddell and Yorkshire Politics', unpublished B.Litt. thesis, University of Oxford, 1976.

4 Another brother, George, inherited lands in Escrick. His descendants lived at Selby and Barlby, where Thomas and Charles Weddell, the latter a shipbuilder and owner, organised the building of Selby Bridge in 1792. Yet another brother was the ancestor of a branch of the family which married into the estate of Waddow Hall. Bedfordshire and Luton Archives and Records Service (BLARS), Lucas Manuscripts L30/14/416/3 and L30/14/416/4; WYAS (Leeds) WYL109/71/26; Baron Frederick Duckham, *The Yorkshire Ouse*, Plymouth, 1967, pp. 75, 203 n. 48.

5 WYAS (Leeds) WYL5013/add.116. The entry for 26 May 1742 in Richard Weddell's account book records: 'To Sundry Accts. Taken out of my wife's hands viz. To Son Tom £8.8.0, To Son William £3.13.6'.

6 *Ibid.*

7 This was almost certainly Dr. Newcome's Academy, for which see R. Fletcher, *The Parkers at Saltram*, London, 1970, p. 133.

8 John Aislabie's sister married Sir William Robinson, Thomas Weddell's cousin and the builder of Newby Park.

9 This relationship is examined, albeit with specific reference to the rather idiosyncratic position of London bankers and merchants by N. Rogers, 'Money, land and lineage: the big bourgeoisie of Hanoverian London,' *Social History*, vol. 4, no. 3, October 1979, pp. 437–454.

10 This was recognised by Daniel Defoe in *The Complete English Tradesman*, London, 1726, p. 376: 'trade in England makes gentlemen. . . for. . . the tradesmen's children, or at least their grandchildren, come to be as good gentlemen, statesmen, Parliament-men, privy-counsellors, judges, bishops, and noblemen, as those of the highest birth and the most antient families.'

11 On this point, see Daniel Defoe, *The Original Power of the Collective Body of the People of England*, London, 1702,

p. 16: 'I make no question but property of land is the best title to government in the world' and Jonathan Swift, *Thoughts on Various Subjects*, Oxford, 1973 (1735) p. 245: 'law in a free country is, or ought to be, the determination of the majority of those who have property in land.'

12 BLARS: Lucas Manuscript L24/284.

13 Walter C. and Gilbert Metcalfe, 'Records of the Family of Metcalfe', 1891, pp. 251–260. Sir William Robinson of Newby Park and Thomas Metcalfe of Nappa were trustees to the marriage settlement of Richard and Barbara Elcock. WYAS (Leeds) WYL5013/2977.

14 Papers connected with Thomas Elcock's Will and the Act of 1777 which enabled the Elcocks to take the surname of Weddell are at WYAS (Leeds) WYL5013/2263.

15 WYAS (Leeds) WYL5013/2264 and 2975.

16 WYAS (Leeds) WYL5013/add.116 and WYL5013/2263/1.

17 WYAS (Leeds) WYL5013/912 and 2203; Northumberland County Record Office. Documents belonging to Mr. H. Blackett, 30 (Newby Hall). William Weddell continued this process when he bought the estate of Sir Thomas Tancred in 1777. BLARS: Lucas Manuscript L30/14/416/1–5; WYAS (Leeds) WYL5013/2277/38.

18 In the years immediately following his uncle's death, Richard Elcock Weddell lived at No. 32 Soho Square, and thereafter in Pall Mall. H. Phillips, *Mid-Georgian London*, London, 1964, p. 298.

19 No in-depth study has been made of building patterns throughout the British Isles but, in a survey undertaken many years ago, Summerson concluded that great houses were supplanted by villas and smaller country houses such as Newby Hall (and Newby Park) over the course of the eighteenth century, while the regional studies of Wilson and Mackley revealed that most houses were remodelled and extended rather than built anew. Most of Yorkshire saw increased building activity in the 1720s–1750s, although their statistics relate to the West Riding. John Summerson, 'The Classical Country House in 18th Century England,' *RSA Journal*, July 1959, pp. 539–587; Wilson and Mackley, *Creating Paradise, op. cit.* pp. 199–232.

20 J. A. Venn, *Alumni Cantabrigienses*, vol. 2, Cambridge, 1954, p. 92 for Richard Elcock and vol. 6, p. 393 for Thomas and William Weddell; WYAS (Leeds) WYL5013/2200. William Weddell's career path was clearly intended to be the law, however, since his father paid his cousin, Alexius Elcock, £2.10.0 'for Law Books for Billy,' in December 1756. WYAS (Leeds) WYL5013/2200.

21 WYAS (Leeds) WYL150/5571 and 13724 and WYL5013/2977. References to Major Weddell in these manuscripts are to Major Charles Weddell of Waddow. Army lists confirm that William Weddell was a Captain in the 3rd West Riding of Yorkshire Militia in 1761. The three West Riding Militia regiments were amalgamated in 1763.

22 Richard Weddell paid Rockingham's servant £3.3.0 'for ffee Commiss.' on June 13 and further payments were recorded in subsequent weeks. WYAS (Leeds) WYL5013/2203.

23 WYAS (Leeds) WYL150/13731.

24 WYAS (Leeds) WYL5013/2886/208.

25 Margaret Weddell appears to have suffered from poor mental and physical health. She never married, although a suitable offer (from her father's standpoint) had been received from a Mr. Garforth c.1748. She remained in her brother's care and, as is often the way with valetudinarians, outlived him by many years. From the 1780s, she lived in Sackville Street, where she died in 1805. WYAS (Leeds) WYL5013/2197b and 2886/222; WYL109, vol. 2c, fol. 32; WYL150/5571.

26 WYAS (Leeds) WYL5013/2839/39 and 2839/40. Why Italy, but apparently not France, was so dangerous a place that such details needed immediate attention is not clear.

27 WYAS (Leeds) WYL5013/2839/43. See also WYL150.

28 WYAS (Leeds) WYL5013/2185. The matter seems to have still been in dispute in 1770.

29 Correspondence between Palgrave and Thomas Gray at this time can be found in Paget Toynbee and Leonard Whibley eds., *Correspondence of Thomas Gray*, Oxford, 1935, pp. 866–868.

30 Evidently aware that Weddell had political aspirations, the Robinsons began to discuss developments amongst themselves although whether they offered any practical advice is a moot point. By 1765, the Newby Hall estate yielded some £7,000 a year, slightly above the average peerage income at this time, and more than enough to support a political career and allow Weddell to move in elevated circles. The next step up would have been a title but surprisingly few new baronetcies were created in Yorkshire during the long eighteenth century. See WYAS (Leeds) WYL150/12272 and 12410 and WYL5013/2839/22 and 2839/37; Wilson and Mackley, *Creating Paradise, op. cit.* pp. 18, 29.

31 WYAS (Leeds) WYL5013/2839/23.

32 For details of the Hull election see Sayer, *William Weddell and Yorkshire Politics, op. cit.* Numerous letters on the subject are at WYAS (Leeds) WYL109, vol. 2a.

33 Accounts of the history and historiography of Rockingham's political career can be found in Paul Langford, *The First Rockingham Administration*, Oxford, 1973 and W. M. Elofson, *The Rockingham Connection and the Second Founding of the Whig Party, 1768–1773*, Montreal, Kingston, London and Buffalo, 1996.

34 Elofson, *The Rockingham Connection and the Second Founding of the Whig Party, op. cit.* p. 16.

35 *Ibid.* p. 24.

36 On the relationship between building activity and political aspiration and achievement, see Wilson and Mackley, *Creating Paradise, op. cit.* p. 201. On Weddell's house in Upper Brook Street, see Jill Low, 'French Taste in London, William Weddell's Town House', *Country Life*, 27 December 1979, pp. 2470–2472. Adam was consulted about alterations to No. 6 Upper Brook Street c.1772 but these were never carried out and it was not until 1787 that Samuel Wyatt was brought in to update the house.

37 On this point, see Wilson and Mackley, *Creating Paradise, op. cit.* p. 68.

38 WYAS (Leeds) WYL5013/2895/3, 2895/8 and 2895/15. During this month, Weddell was also elected a governor of the Foundling Hospital. R. H. Nichols and F. A. Wray, *The History of the Foundling Hospital*, London, 1935, p. 381.

39 Rosemary Baird, *Mistress of the House. Great Ladies and Grand Houses 1670–1830*, London, 2003, p. 13.

40 On this point, see Langford, *The First Rockingham Administration, op. cit.* p. 21. Lady Rockingham was an astute politician who influenced her husband by appealing to his vanity. Langford cites Sheffield Archives Wentworth Woodhouse Muniments (WWM) R168–177, 'If you happen'd to have had the same Idea it would flatter me much more than y[ou]r taking it from me' but numerous other examples can be found in the Rockingham correspondence.

41 Elizabeth Ramsden may not have been Weddell's first romantic attachment; in an anonymous letter addressed to 'Robinson' and bearing the pencilled date of July 1766 (i.e. just after Weddell's return from Italy), the writer reports that 'A Duel was fought last week between a Mr. Weddell Member for Hull and the Duke of Grafton the latter is much blamed it is supposed Mrs. Harris is the occasion for it.' British Library Additional Manuscript 48, 218, fol. 18.

42 WYAS (Leeds) WYL150/145573, 14558 and 14589.

43 Lady Rockingham was perhaps closer to her half-sisters than her half-brother, Sir John Ramsden, but eventually all were absorbed into the Rockingham circle.

44 Elizabeth Ramsden brought a marriage portion of £10,000, annuities of £1,000 and land in Holbeck and Wortley, near Leeds. Weddell's friends, Harry Duncombe of Copgrove and Daniel Lascelles of Goldsborough Hall were the trustees. WYAS (Leeds) WYL109, RA/S 7.

45 WYAS (Leeds) WYL109, vol. 2c, fol. 4/2.

46 *Ibid.* fol. 4/1.

47 Sheffield Archives WWM R168/44/1: 'I got here [Byram Park] on Thursday Evening after dining at Foulston in my way, & that Nights post brought me another letter from you full of descriptions of Audley end in the same stile as Mine from Newby, & no Wonder since the great Mr Adams was the common Father of the Elegance of both those Houses from Newby.' Unfortunately Lady Rockingham's earlier letter describing the alterations at Newby Hall is untraced.

48 *Ibid.* R168/153.

49 On this point, see WYAS (Leeds) WYL109, vol. 2c, fols. 42 and 44. Extracts of William Weddell's political speeches survive in his wife's hand, but it was Lady Rockingham who requested complete copies for her own records. See WYAS (Leeds) WYL109, vol. 2a, fol. 84: 'I have but a moment to save the Post, but I must seize that moment to offer you, (not flattering Compliments) but sincere congratulations, upon the credit & applause that Mr Weddell gain'd at York on Thursday, by the incomparable speech he gave them at the Meeting: our Mr Dixon call'd on purpose to tell me of it, & was so full of it, that he could speak of nothing else, & very much hopes it will appear in Print, he said he thought he had never heard a more thorough good speech, & that Mr Weddell's voice was quite strong & well heard. Mr Hunter arrived [on?] an Echo to ask this, & Ld John Cavendish whose taste & judgment is more to be relied on, confirm'd the whole. As Mr Weddell has what he said on paper I do insist upon your stealing that Paper. In short my Dr Mrs Weddell I do believe I am nearly as much pleased as you are & I long to see you to talk all over. . .'

50 WYAS: WYL109, vol. 2a, fol. 54/1. See also Sir Lewis Namier and John Brooke, *The House of Commons, 1754–1790*, London, 1964, vol. III, p. 617.

51 *Ibid.* fol. 54/2.

52 G. E. Mingay, *English Landed Society in the Eighteenth Century*, London, 1963, p. 261–262; E. P. Thompson, 'The Peculiarities of the English', in R. Miliband and J. Savile eds., *The Socialist Register*, 1965, p. 323.

53 Weddell's full speech is at WYAS (Leeds) WYL109, vol. 2a, fols. 82ff. On 12 September 1780 he wrote to Rockingham, 'I cannot but wish most sincerely well to my friend and neighbour upon this occasion, and think it a proper spirit for ye County to shew at this time, but I must own I hope I may look upon him as chosen (if he be chosen) by ye sense of the county at large and not from ye absolute nomination of that particular community who advertised for ye meeting.' WYAS (Leeds) WYL109, vol. 2a, fol. 81.

54 Elizabeth Weddell's elegy to her brother-in-law is WYAS (Leeds) WYL109, vol. 2a, fol. 105.

55 This was a disastrous election for Rockingham's supporters and a Pyrrhic victory for the Association as no parliamentary reform resulted.

56 WYAS (Leeds) WYL109, vol. 2c, fol. 64.

57 BLARS Lucas Manuscript L30/15/66/164.

58 *The Gentleman's Magazine*, vol. LXII, May 1792, p. 481.

The Newby Hall Drawings
William Connor

1 I am much indebted to many friends and colleagues for sharing their thoughts about these drawings, but particularly to Terry Friedman, who has been immensely generous in this respect and has put the fruits of his research at my disposal.

2 Hugh Honour, 'Newby Hall, Yorkshire', *The Connoisseur*, vol. 134, 1954, pp. 246–251, where he reproduces Adam's design for the study WYAS (Leeds) WYL5013/D1/10/1 and refers to a plan for the sculpture gallery heating system which cannot now be identified; John Cornforth, 'The Making of the Saltram Landscape', *Country Life*, 14 September 1967, pp. 594–597; John Harris, *Catalogue of the Drawings Collection of the Royal Institute of British Architects: Colen Campbell*, Farnborough, Hants, 1973, p. 8; the initial discovery of the Campbell drawings was made by Dr. Lindsay Boynton in 1966 (Howard E. Stutchbury, *The Architecture of Colen Campbell*, Manchester, 1967, pp. 168–169); Geoffrey Beard, *The Work of Robert Adam*, 1978, plates 104 and 105; John Harris, *William Chambers, Knight of the Polar Star*, 1970, plate 75, reproduces a drawing for Newby Park from this collection WYAS (Leeds)WYL 5013/D/4/3/7, which Dr. Low has since attributed to William Belwood; Jill Irene Low, 'The Art and Architectural Patronage of William Weddell (1736–1792) of Newby Hall and his Circle', unpublished PhD thesis, Department of Fine Art, University of Leeds, 1981 (henceforth Low thesis), and her 'William Belwood: Architect and Surveyor', *Yorkshire Archaeological Journal* (henceforth YAJ) vol. 56 (1984), p. 143n. John Harris also reproduces some of the drawings for a pheasantry WYAS (Leeds) WYL5013/D/1/18 and for Grantham House in Whitehall WYAS (Leeds) WYL5013/D/6/1. Christopher Hussey (*Country Life*, vol. 81, 1937, pp. 658–664, 688–693) relies on Arthur T. Bolton, *The Architecture of Robert and James Adam* (1922), who refers only to the drawings in the Sir John Soane's Museum. John Cornforth's 1967 reference to drawings by Thomas Robinson of Rokeby is probably an understandable confusion with Thomas Robinson, 2nd Baron Grantham.

3 John Cornforth, 'Newby Hall, North Yorkshire–I', *Country Life*, 7 June 1979, pp. 1802–1806; Low thesis, *op. cit.*, pp. 3-12. Dr. Low has established that William's elder brother died in 1756.

4 Lindsay Boynton, 'Newby Park, the First Palladian Villa in England', in H. Colvin and J. Harris, eds., *The Country Seat: Studies in the History of the British Country House presented to Sir John Summerson*, 1970, pp. 97–105; J. I. Low, YAJ, *op. cit.*, pp. 143–148.

5 Diary of Henry Vyner 1832–1859, quoted in the preface to the West Yorkshire Archive Service catalogue of WYL5013, but its present location is unknown.

6 The Vyner of Studley Royal Archives at WYAS (Leeds) are under the reference WYL150 (formerly VR).

7 See note 2 above. John Harris (1973) suggests that these Campbell drawings may have been acquired by the 3rd Baron Grantham, Earl de Grey. He may also have acquired another item in the collection with an obscure provenance, namely the design by John Christmas for the Hawtrey monument in St Martin's Church, Ruislip WYAS (Leeds) WYL5013/D/7/1/1. It is discussed and reproduced by Adam White in

'A Biographical Dictionary of London Tomb Sculptors c.1560–c.1660', *Walpole Society*, vol. 61 (1999), pp. 22–23, fig. 1. A further item, possibly never in this collection, but formerly in the possession of Mr. Henry Vyner, is William Townsend's design for the hall and chapel wing in the front quadrangle of The Queen's College, Oxford, and which is now in the Paul Mellon Collection. (John Harris, *Catalogue of British Drawings for Architecture, Decoration, Sculpture and Landscape Gardening in American Collections*, New Jersey, 1971, p. 260). I am indebted to Dr. Terry Friedman for drawing my attention to this last item.

8 Cumbria County Record Office, Whitehaven: Pennington-Ramsden Archives. The ceiling design is reproduced in Geoffrey Beard, *op. cit.*, 1978, colour plate 32.

9 WYAS (Leeds) WYL109/Rockingham 2(c) and 3(b). The former reference prefix was RA.

10 Bedfordshire County Record Office: De Grey of Wrest Park Archives 1487, 1489, L30/13-19, L33/269-281); Low, thesis, *op. cit.*, p. 73. Further drawings for Grantham House by Chambers' assistant, John Yenn, will be found at Delaware University Library (Harris, *op. cit.*, 1971, pp. 314–316).

11 This diaspora is set out in The Royal Commission on Historical Manuscripts, *Guides to Sources for British History 10 and 11: Principal Family and Estate Collections*, 1996, under the entries for De Grey, Barons Lucas, Robinson, Marquises of Ripon, and Vyner of Gautby and Newby.

12 Whilst engaged on the Church of Christ the Consoler 1871–1877, Burges also designed gates and garden terraces, including an unexecuted conservatory WYAS (Leeds) WYL 5013/D/1/22/1-4 and D/15/1. There is also a set of drawings for the church which were not acquired by the WYAS (see John Cornforth, 'Newby in the 19th Century', *Country Life*, 25 December 1980, p. 2408, and J. Mordaunt Crook ed., *The Strange Genius of Willam Burges, 'Art-Architect', 1827–1881*, exhibition catalogue for the National Museum of Wales, Cardiff, and the Victoria and Albert Museum, London, 1981, p. 101. The only significant alteration to Newby Hall in this period took place after Lady Mary's death with the construction of a billiard room above Earl de Grey's dining room in 1892–1894. The architects for this were Walker and Strong of Liverpool, but there are no surviving drawings WYAS (Leeds) WYL5013 addl. 155.

13 All three drawings WYAS (Leeds) WYL5013/D/5/2/1-3 are attributed to Borra by Dr. Low, but D/5/2/4 is actually inscribed 'Borra del.' in Grantham's hand. She suggests that the fountain designs (D/2/5) are copies brought to Turin by Juvarra earlier in the century and passed on to Grantham by Borra (Low thesis, *op. cit.*, p. 85 and n. 315). For the related drawings in Rome see Paolo Marconi, Angela Cipriani and Enrico Valeriani, *I disegni di architettura dell'Archivio storico dell'Academia di San Luca*, Rome, 1974, plates 155–173.

14 Only the chapel appears to have been executed (John Cornforth, 'The Making of the Saltram Landscape', *loc. cit.*).

15 WYAS (Leeds) WYL5013/D/8/1; Harris 1973, p. 8. A stray from this series, also formerly in the possession of Henry Vyner of Studley Royal, being a design for the plasterwork of a rotunda, is now in the Paul Mellon Collection (Harris 1971 p. 322). In 1981 Mr. Vyner also possessed a drawing attributed to Campbell for a chimneypiece at Waverley Abbey, where John Aislabie was building in the late 1720s (Stutchbury, 1967, pp. 66–67). A photocopy of this drawing is available WYAS (Leeds) WYL150/Z 54, but the present location of the original is unknown.

16 Sir Edwin Lutyens described a working drawing as 'merely a letter to a builder telling him precisely what is required of

him' (Royal Institute of British Architects Library, Manuscripts and Archives Collection: LuT/1/3/2, quoted in Eleanor Gawne, 'Cataloguing Architectural Drawings', *Journal of the Society of Archivists*, vol. 24 no. 2, October 2003, p. 176).

17 WYAS (Leeds) WYL5013/D/1/6/12. Both Robert Adam and Sir William Chambers would sometimes place a perfectly measured drawing within a landscape perspective (A. A. Tait, *Robert Adam: Drawings and Imagination*, Cambridge 1993, pp. 177–178, fig. 111; Giles Worsley, 'Chambers and Architectural Draughtsmanship' in *Sir William Chambers, Architect to George III*, ed. John Harris and Michael Snodin, New Haven and London, 1996, pp. 186–191 and plate 274).

18 *Country Life*, 21 June 1979, p. 2009. Chambers trained his assistants to follow his style even to the extent of imitating his handwriting (Giles Worsley, *op. cit.*, 1996, p. 189).

19 WYAS (Leeds) WYL5013/D/1/7/9 and 10; Arthur T. Bolton, 1922, pp. 137 and 140, where he quotes from the Reverend Richard Warner, *Tour Thro' the Northern Counties*, Bath 1802, p. 137. Warner refers to 'a dim religious light' and 'the magic effect with which the mind is impressed when we look through the door at the opposite extremity' (i.e. into the sculpture gallery). 'Here we throw a glance into the penetralia of the temple'.

20 WYAS (Leeds) WYL5013/D/3/1–13. The house, which was demolished in 1936, is illustrated and discussed in *Survey of London*, vol. 39 (1977) p. 121, pl. 17(d) and vol. 40 (1980) pp. 201–203, pl. 55(c); Jill Low, 'French Taste in London', *Country Life*, 27 December 1979, p. 2470–2472. Both the plate warmer and the urns are illustrated and discussed in Eileen Harris, *The Genius of Robert Adam His Interiors*, New Haven and London, 2001, p. 224.

21 WYAS (Leeds) WYL5013/D/3/1/14. James Wyatt also worked for the Vyner family at their London house in Conduit Street. So the carriage may possibly have been for them (Colvin, *Dictionary, op. cit.*, p. 1120).

22 WYAS (Leeds) WYL5013/D/1/21/2–5.

23 WYAS (Leeds) WYL5013/D/1/1/3/10. Miss Hartley was the daughter of David Hartley the philosopher and sister of David Hartley the younger, statesman, inventor and MP for Hull. See *The Dictionary of National Biography* and WYAS (Leeds) WYL109 Rockingham Correspondence 2c, pp. 116–124, where Miss Hartley writes from Belvedere and Chislehurst in Kent 1790–1794 referring, amongst other things, to the artistic circle there.

24 WYAS (Leeds) WYL5013/D/4/2/11–13.

25 *Ibid.* 1/2/1-2

26 Colvin, Dictionary, *op. cit.*, pp. 431–433.

27 WYAS (Leeds) WYL5013/D/2/1/1; 2/1/5

28 *Ibid.* 1/2/12-15; 12/2/1-4.

29 *Ibid.* 1/18/1-6

30 *Ibid.* 9/1-3: Terence R Leach and Robert Pacey, *Lost Lincolnshire Country Houses*, vol. 4, Burgh le Marsh 1993, pp. 16–34.

31 *Ibid.* 1/22 and WYAS (Leeds) WYL5013/D/15/1-2.

32 WYAS (Leeds) WYL5013/2403

33 *Ibid.* 2436

34 *Ibid.* 2411

35 *Ibid.* 2412A

36 *Ibid.* 2382

37 *Ibid.* 2328. Lindsay Boynton, 1970, *op. cit.*, p. 104 n. 26.

38 *Ibid.* 2384A; Royal Commission on Historical Monuments: York vol. 4 (1975), p. 36.

39 WYAS (Leeds) WYL5013/2007. The accommodation was approached via a porter's lodge and included a great hall,

great stairs, great parlour, withdrawing room, common hall, little parlour, kitchen, buttery, stable and coach house. There was an entry to the back yard from Sherbourne Lane. The site is shown clearly in T. F. Reddaway, *The Rebuilding of London After the Great Fire*, 1940, plate 32 and partly on plate 33.

40 WYAS (Leeds) WYL5013/D/1/1/1; WYL5013/2399; WYL5013/D/ 1/22/1–4; WYL5013/D/1.

41 WYAS (Leeds) WYL5013/D/1/1/4. It was published in Joannes Kip, *Nouveau Théâtre de la Grande Bretagne*, London 1724–1725 (5 vols in 3), vol. 1, pl. 53 and is reproduced in the current Newby Hall guidebook.

42 WYAS (Leeds) Ingilby of Ripley Archives (WYL 230) add. acc. 2922/44. Aram's career is discussed and this design reproduced in Peter Aram, *A Practical Treatise of Flowers*, ed. Frank Felsenstein, Proceedings of the Leeds Philosophical and Literary Society, Literary and Historical Section, vol. 20 pt. 1 (Leeds 1985), p. [121] 87. The painting is reproduced in the Newby Hall guidebook.

43 WYAS (Leeds) WYL5013/D/1/22/10, 13–14. One of these is the illustration of the exterior of Newby reproduced in Eileen Harris, *The Genius of Robert Adam, op. cit.*, pl. 312. The chimneys had been removed before the *Country Life* photographs were taken for Christopher Hussey in 1937.

44 WYAS (Leeds) WYL5013/D/1/22/12. Another photograph of the library at this time is reproduced in John Cornforth, 'Newby in the 19th Century', *Country Life*, 25 December 1980, p. 2408.

45 The Buckler album contains various views of Newby made between 1805 and 1817. It is in the Paul Mellon Collection (John Harris, *op. cit.*, 1971, p. 40). For the *Country Life* photographs see Christopher Hussey, *Country Life, op. cit.*, 1937.

Taste, Travel and the Reform of Culture in the 1760s
Martin Myrone

1 George Birkbeck Hill ed., *Boswell's Life of Johnson*, 6 vols, Oxford, 1934–1950, vol. 3, p. 36 (11 April 1776).

2 Thus the portraits he commissioned did not join an extended sequence of images of distinguished forebears, as would be the case in so many households founded on older wealth. On the importance of context for elite portraits, see Kate Retford, 'Sensibility and Genealogy in the Eighteenth Century Family Portrait: The Collection at Kedleston Hall', *The Historical Journal* 46:3, 2003, pp. 533–60 and 'Reynolds's Portrait of Mrs Theresa Parker: A Case Study in Context', *The British Art Journal 4:3*, 2004, pp. 80–86. The mystery which surrounds the intended location of Weddell's Grand Tour portraits, which may have been destined for his London house or Newby Hall, may in this context be telling: in neither would they have had a meaningful genealogical setting.

3 See, variously: Michèle Cohen, *Fashioning Masculinity: National Identity and Language in the Eighteenth Century*, London and New York, 1996, pp. 54–63; Bruce Redford, *Venice & the Grand Tour*, New Haven and London, 1996, pp. 14–15. Robin Eagles, *Francophilia in English Society, 1748–1815*, Basingstoke, 2000, pp. 120–1; Katherine Turner, *British Travel Writers in Europe: Authorship, Gender and National Identity*, Aldershot, 2001, pp. 2–3; Jean Viviès, trans. Claire Davison, *English Travel Narratives in the Eighteenth Century: Exploring Genres*, Aldershot, 2002, pp. 25–6.

4 This is, essentially, to extend Jill Low's arguments that Weddell's cultural patronage needs to be considered as closely integrated with his social and political aspirations and related to larger

changes in British culture. Her 'The Art and Architectural Patronage of William Weddell (1736–1792) of Newby Hall and His Circle', unpublished PhD thesis, University of Leeds, 1981. This lucidly argued and extensively documented study remains the essential foundation for any consideration of Weddell and Newby Hall.

5 Kay Dian Kriz, 'The Grand Tour', *Eighteenth Century Studies, 31*, 1997–8, pp. 87–89.

6 A fundamental statement of Bourdieu's method is to be found in his *Outline of a Theory of Practice*, trans. Richard Nice, Cambridge, 1977, but most pertinent is his monumental evisceration of the conventional fallacies surrounding aesthetic judgement, *Distinction: A Social Critique of the Judgement of Taste*, trans. Richard Nice, London, 1984, and a collection of his essays, Randal Johnson ed., *The Field of Cultural Production: Essays on Art and Literature*, Cambridge, 1993. The pertinence of Bourdieu's work for the analysis of the Grand Tour has been suggested by Nigel Llewellyn, 'Those Loose and Immodest Pieces: Italian Art and the British Point of View' in Shearer West ed., *Italian Culture in Northern Europe in the Eighteenth Century*, Cambridge, 1999, pp. 67–100 (p. 70).

7 See these suggestive comments: 'I think the Duke of Dorset improved by his travels, he has laid our 6 or 7000 with Jenkins, & virtu has furnished him with more ideas & conversation' John Fitzpatrick, 2nd Earl of Ossory to Thomas Robinson, 1st Baron Grantham, 15 September 1771, Bedfordshire and Luton Record Office, L 30/14/138/1; 'My Virtù has received some little addition from Jenkins in the way of exchange last summer': William Weddell to Thomas Robinson, 21 January 1777, Bedfordshire and Luton Record Office, L 30/14/416/2.

8 John, Lord Sheffield, ed., *Edward Gibbon: Memoirs of my Life and Writings* (1796), reprint ed. A. Cockshut, J. Cockshut and Stephen Constantine, Keele University Press, 1996, p. 145.

9 Richard Lassels, 'A Preface to the Reader Concerning Travelling' (1670) in *An Italian Voyage, Or, A Compleat Journey Through Italy, 'Second Edition with large Additions, by a Modern hand'*, 2 parts, London, 1698. On Lassels see Edward Chaney, *The Grand Tour and the Great Rebellion: Richard Lassels and 'The Voyage of Italy' in the Seventeenth Century*, Geneva, 1985.

10 See Robert Donald Spector, *English Literary Periodicals and the Climate of Opinion During the Seven Years' War*, The Hague, 1966, pp. 62–5; also Robert Donald Spector, 'The Connoisseur: A Study of the Functions of a Persona' in John H. Middendorf ed., *English Writers of the Eighteenth Century*, New York and London, 1971, pp. 109–121, and Lance Bertelsten, *The Nonsense Club: Literature and Popular Culture 1749–1764*, Oxford, 1986. For more wide-ranging accounts of the patriotic feeling in these years see Gerald Newman, *The Rise of English Nationalism: A Cultural History, 1740–1830* 1987, rev. edn. Basingstoke, 1997; Linda Colley, *Britons: Forging the Nation, 1707–1837*, New Haven and London, 1992; and Kathleen Wilson, *The Sense of the People: Politics, Culture and Imperialism in England 1715–1785*, Cambridge, 1995.

11 Richard Hurd, *Dialogues on the Uses of Foreign Travel: Considered as Part of an English Gentleman's Education: Between Lord Shaftesbury and Mr Locke*, London, 1764, pp. 43–6, p. 71. Cohen, *Fashioning Masculinity, op. cit.*, pp. 58-63, discusses this text in some detail. We can note that Hurd was known and appreciated in Weddell's circle: in 1764 the young Frederick Robinson reported to Thomas Robinson that he had been reading Hurd's *Moral and Political Dialogues* as an antidote to Hume's controversial *History of England*; see

his letter of 19 February 1764, Bedfordshire and Luton Archives and Records Services, Wrest Park (Lucas) Manuscripts L 30/14/333/14.

12 Bound volume, description of travels in Holland and France 1763, Cumbria Record Office and Local Studies Library, Whitehaven, D/Pen/221.

13 Thomas Robinson to Frederick Robinson, 14 October 1759, WYAS (Leeds) WYL150/6032 (12307).

14 Thomas Robinson to Beilby Porteus, 23 February 1760, Bedfordshire and Luton Archives and Records Services, Wrest Park (Lucas) Manuscripts L 30/14/315/23.

15 See Chard, *Pleasure and Guilt on the Grand Tour, op. cit.*

16 Thomas Robinson to Thomas Robinson 1st Baron Grantham, 23 March 1760, WYAS (Leeds) WYL150/6032 (12232).

17 To indulge in 'delusion' in this way was something most fully discussed and analysed in relation to the aesthetics of the Sublime, which was the subject of intense scrutiny in precisely these years. The literature on these topics is considerable, and Chard in particular considers the connection with the Grand Tour, but also relevant is the discussion of the pleasures of 'delusion' in E. J. Clery, *The Rise of Supernatural Fiction, 1762–1800*, Cambridge, 1995.

18 Thomas Robinson to Thomas Robinson 1st Baron Grantham, 24 January 1760, WYAS (Leeds) WYL150/6032 (12314).

19 Thomas Robinson to Thomas Robinson, 1st Baron Grantham, 9 August 1760, WYAS (Leeds) WYL150/ 6032 (12325); this important letter printed and discussed in 'Batoni and Mengs', *Leeds Art Calendar 44*, 1960, pp. 23–4. See also Thomas Robinson to Thomas Robinson, 1st Baron Grantham, 21 June 1760, on first encountering the work of Mengs and Batoni and contrasting the 'very strong & chaste' qualities of the German with the 'more glaring' and less forceful work of the Italian WYAS (Leeds) WYL150/ 6032 (12322).

20 Thomas Robinson to Thomas Robinson, 1st Baron Grantham, 15 May 1763, WYAS (Leeds) WYL150/6032 (12296).

21 L. A. de Caraccioli, *Voyage de la raison en Europe* (1771) quoted in Frances Acomb, *Anglophobia in France 1763–1789: An Essay in the History of Constitutionalism and Nationalism*, Durham NC, 1950, p. 11.

22 Notably Baron de Grimm, *Correspondence littéraire* dated 1 May 1763, in Svend Erikson, trans. and ed. Peter Thornton, *Early Neo-Classicism in France: The Creation of the Louis Seize Style in Architectural Decoration, Furniture and Ormolu, Gold and Silver, and Sèvres Porcelain in the Mid-Eighteenth Century*, London, 1974, pp. 264–5, and discussed on pp. 48–51. For a general account of cultural reform see Albert Boime, *Art in an Age of Revolution 1750–1800*, Chicago and London, 1987, esp. pp. 55–183

23 In 1766, Thomas Gray joked that the typical activities of Yorkshire society would involve 'riding & walking with Mr Aislaby, singing Duets with my cousin Fanny, improving with Mr Weddell, conversing with Mr Harry Duncomb'; letter to Norton Nicholls, 26 August 1766, in Paget Toynbee and Leonard Whibley, *Correspondence of Thomas Gray* (1935), reprint 3 vols., Oxford, 1971, vol. 3, p. 928. 'Improvement' was, then, very much Weddell's element.

24 Louis XVI's own estimate was that 40,000 Englishmen had travelled through Calais in the period 1763–5, while a newspaper report of August 1763 suggested that 7,400 passports had been issued so far that year – an enormous figure, and it is worth remembering too that passports were not strictly necessary for travel at this time, anyway. See Black, *France and the Grand Tour, op. cit.*, also Eagles, *Francophilia, op. cit.*, pp. 120-1.

25 This also corresponds to the values of probity and modesty

that Low detects in Weddell's political career, and his commitment to Whig values, see Low, 'The Art and Architectural Patronage of William Weddell', *op. cit.*, vol. 1, p. 525.

26 David Hume to Isaac Barré, 16 July 1764, in Raymond Klibansky and Ernest C. Mossner eds., *New Letters of David Hume*, Oxford, 1954, p. 85; Francis Griffin Stokes ed., *A Journal of my Journey to Paris in the Year 1765 by the Rev. William Cole*, London, 1931, p. 1; Laurence Sterne to John-Hall Stevenson, 19 May 1764, in Lewis Perry Curtis ed., *Letters of Laurence Sterne*, Oxford, 1935, p. 213.

27 Edward Gibbon to Dorothea Gibbon, 25 March 1763, in J. E. Norton ed., *The Letters of Edward Gibbon*, 3 vols., London, 1956, vol. 1, pp. 139–40.

28 Edith Pelham ed., *Mrs Bousquet's Diary* (1765), Norwich, 1927, p. 45.

29 We could note that Horace Walpole made a combined visit to Jean de Julienne's collection and the Gobelins, see his Paris journal, entry for 18 December 1765, W. S. Lewis ed., *The Yale Edition of Horace Walpole's Correspondence*, 48 vols., New Haven, 1937–1983, vol. 7. On the Boucher-Neilson tapestries see Edith A. Standen, 'Croome Court: The Tapestries', *The Metropolitan Museum of Art Bulletin 18*, 1959–60, pp. 91–111; Eileen Harris, 'Robert Adam and the Gobelins', *Apollo 76*, March–July 1962, pp. 100–6; Eileen Harris, 'The Moor Park Tapestries', *Apollo 86*, September 1967, pp. 180–9; Low, 'The Art and Architectural Patronage of William Weddell', *op. cit.*, vol. 1, pp. 375–395; Gervase Jackson-Stops ed., *The Treasure Houses of Britain: Five Hundred Years of Private Patronage and Art Collecting*, National Gallery of Art, Washington 1985, cat. 259; Eileen Harris, *The Genius of Robert Adam His Interiors*, New Haven and London, 2001, pp. 212–231.

30 Tobias Smollett, ed., Frank Felsentein, *Travels Through France and Italy* (1766), Oxford 1979, p. 47 (Paris, '12 October 1763').

31 The zoologist and traveller Thomas Pennant noted that Gobelins tapestries were 'excessive dear' and 'very dear': G. R. de Beer ed., *Thomas Pennant: Tour on the Continent 1765*, London, 1948 (pp. 23–4, 20 March 1765 and p. 25, 22 March 1765).

32 Weddell had been informed about his sister's ill health by Christmas 1763; see Weddell to Thomas Robinson, 1st Baron Grantham, 25 December 1763, WYAS (Leeds) WYL 5013/2338/47. Grantham wrote on 9 January 1764, noting that Weddell 'need not be absent from Paris above three weeks at most' so he would 'be able to continue your journey from thence towards Italy without stopping upon your return to France' (WYAS (Leeds) WYL5013/ 2839/39). On 22 January, Weddell wrote to Grantham saying that 'I hope to have ye Honour of paying my respects to your Lordship at Whitehall at ye beginning of next month' (WYAS (Leeds) WYL5013/2839/43).

33 Palgrave was recalled as 'a person of small stature, neat in his appearance, agreeable and clever in conversation, and a very pleasant companion. He was much esteemed by the parishioners at Palgrave, charitable to the poor, and performed with care the duties of his parish. A little irregularity was given to his figure by his head being drawn aside towards the shoulder, which was the occasion of a ludicrous circumstance still remembered in his parish happening to him from a fall when hunting'; this from the reminiscences of Rev. William Aldeson, in Rev. John Mitford ed., *The Correspondence of Thomas Gray and William Mason*, London, 1853, pp. 158–160nn. As a friend of Thomas Gray, Palgrave has received notice, though never very probing, from the poet's modern biographers, most recently Robert L. Mack, *Thomas Gray: A Life*, New Haven and London, 2000, p. 487 and *passim*.

34 It was reported by Thomas Gray on 13 October 1764 that Palgrave was at Geneva, and 'that he has pass'd a fortnight in the Paris de Vaux, & the Cantons of Bern, Fribourg & Soleurre, & return'd by the Lake of Neufchatel'; letter to James Brown, in *Correspondence of Thomas Gray, op. cit.*, vol. 2, pp. 844-845.

35 In March 1765 Gray was advising Palgrave and Weddell to 'strike out of the beaten path of English travellers, and see a little of the country' and giving detailed instructions on what to look out for in Paris on the return journey; see *Correspondence of Thomas Gray, op. cit.*, vol. 2, pp. 866–8. In his letter to James Grant, 5 June 1765, Jenkins said that Palgrave and Weddell had left Rome 'some weeks since'; National Archives of Scotland, GD 248/49/3/24.

36 Jules David Prown, 'A Course of Antiquities at Rome, 1764', in *Eighteenth Century Studies 31*, 1997–8, pp. 90–100, details a closely contemporary tour of Rome in the spring of 1764, undertaken by Weddell's American peers Samuel Powel and John Morgan under the instruction of James Byres.

37 In his letter to James Grant, 5 June 1765, Jenkins thanks him and Robinson for their 'kind recommendation of me to Mr Weddell'; National Archives of Scotland, GD 248/49/3/24.

38 On Hamilton and his work see: David Irwin, 'Gavin Hamilton: Archaeologist, Painter, and Dealer' in *Art Bulletin 44*, 1962, pp. 87–102; Nicola Kalinsky, 'Gavin Hamilton and the Genesis of Neo-Classical History Painting', unpublished MA Report, Courtauld Institute of Art, 1985; Julia Lloyd Williams, *Gavin Hamilton 1723–1798*, Edinburgh, 1994.

39 On the increasing prevalence of the idea of the Bolognese reform of art see Mahon, *Studies in Seicento Art and Theory*, pp. 212-7; on Reni's reputation see D. Stephen Pepper, *Guido Reni: A Complete Catalogue of his Works with an Introductory Text*, Oxford, 1984, pp. 45–9.

40 However, at the end of his Tour Weddell did purchase a substantial subject-painting by Mengs from Jenkins, *The Holy Family with St Elizabeth and St John the Baptist*. See Steffi Roettgen, *Anton Raphael Mengs 1728–1779 and his British Patrons*, London, 1993, cat. 19.

41 Llewellyn, 'Those Loose and Immodest Pieces' *op. cit.*, pp. 70–1; Black, *Italy and the Grand Tour, op. cit.*, p. 7 illustrates the Weddell group portrait as exemplary of the genre.

42 See Francis Haskell and Nicholas Penny, *Taste and the Antique: the Lure of Classical Sculpture 1500–1900*, New Haven and London, 1981, pp. 184–7; Anthony M. Clark, ed. Edgar Peters Bowron, *Pompeo Batoni: A Complete Catalogue of his Works with an Introductory Text*, Oxford, 1985, cats. 291–3.

43 See Clark, *Pompeo Batoni, op. cit.*, for the portraits of Charles John Crowle (cat. 240), Thomas Dundas (cat. 278), Count Kirill Grigorjewitsch Raxumovsky (cat. 299), John, 3rd Baron Monson (cat. 375) and Thomas Coke (cat. 377).

44 Richard Warner, *A Tour Through the Northern Counties of England and the Borders of Scotland*, 2 vols., Bath 1802, vol. 1, p. 253.

45 Sheffield ed., *Edward Gibbon: Memoirs of my Life and Writings* (1796), *op. cit.*, p. 172 and 172n. Sheffield (1735–1821) had travelled in Italy with his companion and fellow Roman Club member Major Richard Ridley (1736–89) in 1764–5. The other members listed by Sheffield are Thomas Charles Bigge (c.1739–94) educated at Oxford; William Guise (1737–83) educated at Oxford and Lincoln's Inn; John Aubrey (1739–1826), a student at Westminster and Oxford, and his travelling companion the Rev. William Cleaver (1742–1815),

an Oxonian; Lord Montstuart (1744–1814), educated at Harrow and Winchester who had travelled with his governor James Edmonstone (born c.1720); John Damer (1744–1776) and his brother George (1746–1808) both educated at Eton and Cambridge; Sir Thomas Gascoigne, 8th Bart. (1745–1810), a Catholic educated outside of the English system; Willoughby Bertie, 4th Earl of Abingdon (1740–1799), schooled at Westminster and Oxford, and his brother Peregrine Bertie (1741–90) also a former Westminster; Godfrey Bagnall Clarke (c.1742–74); Frederick Augustus, 5th Earl of Berkeley (1744–1810); John Hort (1735–1807), educated at Trinity College, Dublin.

46 This may be contrary to the claims made by, for instance, Redford, *Venice & the Grand Tour, op. cit.*, p. 15; Arnold, 'The Illusion of Grandeur?', *op. cit.*, p. 103 and Turner, *British Travel Writers in Europe, op. cit.*, pp. 58–9, who each argue that the Grand Tour functioned as a kind of substitute for university education. The general educational, generational social profile exhibited in the membership of the Roman Club can be detected among Gavin Hamilton's other patrons. Consider, for instance, the six patrons of his canvases depicting scenes from the *Iliad*: Charles Compton, 7th Earl of Northampton (1737–63); Henry Temple, 2nd Viscount Palmerston (1739–1802); Luke Gardiner (1745–98); Douglas, 8th Duke of Hamilton (1756–99); and Robinson's particular friends James Grant of Grant (1738–1811) and Francis Russell, Lord Tavistock (1739–67). Three of these men had been schooled at Westminster; and two at Eton; the earliest education of the sixth, Palmerston, is not recorded, but he had been to Cambridge, like three others. Only Compton had instead been to Oxford, and only the Duke of Hamilton had not been to university at all. The only major exception to the aristocratic and landed background of Gavin Hamilton's major patrons was the wealthy merchant John Boyd; see David Hancock, *Citizens of the World: London Merchants and the Integration of the British Atlantic Community, 1735–1785*, Cambridge, 1995, pp. 437–443.

47 Weddell joined the militia in 1759 and served as a captain in the north of England throughout the War. See Low, 'The Art and Architectural Patronage of William Weddell', *op. cit.*, vol. 1, pp. 10–1 and vol. 2, p. 535 n. 35.

48 This is the particular theme explored by J. G. A. Pocock, *Barbarism and Religion: The Enlightenments of Edward Gibbon, 1737–1764*, Cambridge 1999, also Eliza G. Gould, *The Persistence of Empire: British Political Culture in the Age of the American Revolution*, Chapel Hill and London, 2000.

49 Sheffield ed., *Edward Gibbon: Memoirs of my Life and Writings* (1796), *op. cit.*, p. 172.

50 Italy provided pleasures other than high culture and high-minded history; the Damers were known for their unruly behaviour, and Gibbon recorded his rather unruly lifestyle in English company in Switzerland in some detail. Things could get out of hand: Gascoigne was with the Damers in Rome during a fracas in which a coachman died (see the article on Gascoigne in Ingamells, *Dictionary of British and Irish Travellers, op. cit.* Gibbon referred to the 'Wicked Company' of Clarke and Damer in a letter to John Holroyd, 29 January 1772 (*Letters of Edward Gibbon, op. cit.*, vol. 1, p. 301). A reference in a letter of the preceding day to 'the Romans' confirms that this was the gathering in question. Of all this group, the unhappiest, seediest fate was that of John Damer, who killed himself in 1776 after spending the evening at Stacey's brothel in Covent Garden, where he 'had two Girls & a blind fiddler, which was his way of passing almost every evening, tho he has never known to fuck any woman', John Crawford to

Robinson, Grafton St., 21 Aug 1776, received 9 September, Bedfordshire and Luton Archives and Records Service, Wrest Park (Lucas) Manuscripts L 30/14/86/4. For the improper aspects of masculine conviviality in the context of Weddell's other club, the Dilettanti, see Shearer West, 'Libertinism and the Ideology of Male Friendship in the Portraits of the Society of Dilettanti', *Eighteenth Century Life*, vol. 16, n.s. 2, May 1992, pp. 76–100

51 For this see David Solkin, *Painting for Money: The Visual Arts and the Public Sphere in Eighteenth Century England*, New Haven and London, 1993.

52 See Seymour Howard, *Bartolomeo Cavaceppi: Eighteenth Century Restorer*, PhD. University of Chicago 1958; published New York and London, 1982, pp. 64–70; also his *Antiquity Restored: Essays on the Afterlife of the Antique*, Vienna, 1990, p. 84 and *passim*.

53 The authenticity of the Cleopatra so proudly displayed in Batoni's portrait of Weddell was doubted by Wincklemann, and was soon after more thoroughly interrogated. See Haskell and Penny, *Taste and the Antique, op. cit.*, p. 187.

54 Warner, *A Tour Through the Northern Counties, op. cit.*, vol. 1, p. 257. On the purchase of the Venus see the sale catalogue *The Jenkins Venus*, Christie's London, 13 June 2002.

55 See Jill Low, 'French Taste in London: William Weddell's Town House', *Country Life*, 27 December 1979, pp. 2470–2.

56 Charles Townley to Thomas Jenkins, 15 July 1779, quoted in Harris, *The Genius of Robert Adam, op. cit.*, p. 219. Such a comment might suggest a bit of defensiveness in comments of Countess of Bute to Mrs. Delany: 'the elegance and magnificence of Mr Weddell's house, all ornamented by Mr Adams, in his highest (and indeed, I think) best taste'.Lady Llanover ed., *The Autobiography and Correspondence of Mary Granville, Mrs Delany*, 6 vols., vol. 6, p. 277–8.

William Weddell and his Architects
Eileen Harris

1 Celia Fiennes, *The Journeys of Celia Fiennes*, ed., Christopher Morris, London, 1947, p. 85; Johannes Kip and Leonard Knyff, *Britannia Illustrata*, London, 1707, I.

2 According to Ely Hargrove, *History of the Castle, Town and Forest of Knaresborough with Harrowgate*, 6th ed., 1821, p. 339, the estate was sold by John Blackett.

3 Will of Thomas Weddell, proved 11 July 1747, PROB 11/756. The sum of £70,000 said by Low to have been laid out on the purchase of land is clearly a mistake. See Jill Low, 'Newby Hall: Two Late Eighteenth Century Inventories', *Furniture History XXII*, 1986.

4 John Carr's extra illustrated copy of the first two volumes of *Vitruvius Britannicus*, now at Fairfax House, Yorkshire, contains loosely inserted sheets of 'The account of the disbursements, chiefly for workmanship made by John Carr for William Weddell Esqr' from 15 January 1764 to 22 August 1764 in a fine hand (not Carr's) and two sheets of accounts in Carr's hand, one dated 1755 for unspecified building. There is no real evidence that any of these accounts relate to Newby. In fact, the elevation and plans for a row of town houses on the verso of the incomplete 1764 Weddell account, suggest that the bills could be related to one of Weddell's properties in York.

5 WYAS (Leeds) WYL150/13633.

6 WYAS (Leeds) WYL5013/D/1/ 3/2. My suggested date, after 1758, is based on letters of March and April 1758 from Richard Weddell to his agent, Mr. Bewley WYAS (Leeds)

WYL5013/2034 concerning the completion of the kitchen which is shown in the plan.

7 14 August 1762 Attorney General Charles Yorke agreed that Thomas Weddell's legacy of £5,000 left to William as younger son could still be vested in him now that he was heir to the whole estate.

8 Eileen Harris, *The Genius of Robert Adam His Interiors*, London, 2001, p. 48.

9 WYAS (Leeds) WYL5013/2839/39.

10 See note 4 above.

11 Letters of 19 and 23 September 1765, WYAS (Leeds) WYL5013/2839/22 and/23.

12 An abortive meeting between Weddell and Stuart was mentioned in a letter from Thomas Gray to William Mason on 23 May 1767. See Paget Toynbee and Leonard Whibley, ed., *Correspondence of Thomas Gray*, Oxford, 1935, letter 440, p. 957. For Stuart and the organ see John Cornforth, 'Newby Hall, Yorkshire – I', *Country Life*, 7 June 1979, p. 1804.

13 Harris, *The Genius of Robert Adam, op. cit.* at note 8 above, p. 227, 357 n 69. WYAS (Leeds) WYL5013/D/1/8/1.

14 Robert Adam to James Adam, re. Harewood. 17 June 1758, SRO GD 18/4848; re. Kedleston, 11 Dec. 1758, SRO Clerk MS 4854.

15 WYAS (Leeds) WYL5013/D/1/6/4. Whether this plan is in Adam's hand or Weddell's (as J. Low maintains), or both is uncertain. The concept is certainly Adam's. See Robin Middleton, 'The Sculpture Gallery at Newby Hall', *AA Files* XIII, 1986, pp. 51–2.

16 Gallery dome WYAS (Leeds) WYL5013/D/1/17/4; SM 11:236,237, the latter dated 1767. Dining-room ceiling WYL5013/D1/ 7/5, signed and dated 1767. Elevations of the north and west walls of the gallery, WYL5013/D/1/6/12 and 14.

17 Richard Warner, *A Tour through the Northern Counties of England and the Borders of Scotland*, Bath, 1802, II, pp. 253–4.

18 *Ibid.*

19 Adam's design for the ceiling of the staircase is dated 1771, SM 11:241.

20 There is a large scale working-drawing by Joseph Rose for the string steps and string board in the Newby Hall Archive, WYAS (Leeds) WYL5013/D/1/12/5.

21 WYAS (Leeds) WYL5013/D/1/12/1,2,3. Jill Low, 'William Belwood: Architect and Surveyor', *The Yorkshire Archaeological Journal*, 1984, LVI, pp. 133–34.

22 Harris, *The Genius of Robert Adam, op. cit.* at note 8 above, p. 231, pl. 346.

23 WYL5013/1/14/1. Low, *loc. cit.* at note 20 above, pp. 134–36, pl. 3.

24 Jill Low, 'French Taste in London William Weddell's Town House', *Country Life*, 27 Dec. 1979, p. 2470, fig.2.

25 WYAS (Leeds) WYL5013/D/1/14/6 'Frieze for over doors in the Principal Lodging Room'. The design is by Adam and was executed. The two bay room is over the south part of the tapestry drawing-room. Low, *loc. cit.*, at note 20 above, p. 136.

26 Design for the hall ceiling, SM 11:238. There is no copy at Newby.

27 WYAS (Leeds) WYL5013/D/1/3/5.

28 Edward Croft-Murray, *Decorative Painting in England, 1537–1837*, London, 1970, II, p. 290, pl. 95. See also John Cornforth, 'Newby Hall, Yorkshire – III', *Country Life*, 21 June 1979, p. 2009 and fig. 10. Two of the painted panels are on doors opening to the principal bedroom to the north and a powdering closet behind the screen in the alcove room; a third opens to a small closet.

29 Giovanni Battista Piranesi, *L'Antichità Romane. . .*, Rome, (1756), III, pl. XLV.

30 Low, William Belwood, *op. cit.*, p. 139.

31 For drawings by Belwood of timber construction see WYAS (Leeds) WYL5013/D/1/6/17,18,19,21 and WYL5013/D/1/7/3.

32 Low, William Belwood, *op. cit.*, p. 139, pl. 7. Cumbria Record Office, D/Penn/Yorkshire houses, Belwood's design for the front of the stables; and three designs signed 'J. Carr'. Arthur T. Bolton illustrated but did not discuss the stables in *The Works of Robert and James Adam*, London, 1922, II, p. 145; Nicholas Pevsner declared the stables to be by Robert Adam, *Yorkshire West Riding*, London, 1967, p. 376

33 Adam designs for the porch on the east front: WYAS (Leeds) WYL 5013/D/1/3/8 and SM 41:73. Belwood's design, WYAS (Leeds) WYL 5031/D/1/3/9. Low, William Belwood, *op. cit.*, p. 139, pl. 5.

34 Low, William Belwood, *op. cit.*, p.139, pl. 139. The idea was evidently suggested by Weddell.

35 *Ibid.* p. 136, pl. 4.

36 *Ibid.* p. 136, note 11.

37 WYAS (Leeds) WYL5031/D/1/10/5,6, Belwood's wall elevations of the library or study with his bookcases. Jill Low, 'Two Late-Eighteenth Century Inventories', *Furniture History*, 1986, XXII, p. 156.

38 WYAS (Leeds) WYL5031/D/1/10/1 is Adam's initial design; WYL5031/D/1/10/2 is his revised version which was executed.

39 This was a hasty assumption of mine, Harris, *The Genius of Robert Adam, op. cit.* at note 8 above, p. 231, pls. 344 and 345, which I wish to correct here. See also Low, *loc. cit.*, at note 20 above, p. 133, pl. 2.

40 Low, William Belwood, *op. cit.*, p. 143, note 28.

The Sculpture Gallery at Newby Hall
Ruth Guilding

1 Susan M. Pearce, *Museums, Objects, Collections*, Leicester and London, 1992, p. 51; John Barrell, 'The Dangerous Goddess: Masculinity, Prestige and the Aesthetic in Early-Eighteenth Century Britain', in *The Birth of Pandora and the Division of Knowledge*, London, 1992, p. 63.

2 M. J. Sayer, 'William Weddell and Yorkshire Politics', B.Litt. thesis, Pembroke College, University of Oxford, 1976, abstract.

3 John Ingamells, *A Dictionary of English and Irish Travellers in Italy 1701–1800*, London and New York, 1997, p. 286.

4 Robert W. Jones, *Gender and the Formation of Taste in Eighteenth Century Britain*, Cambridge, 1998, p. vii; Barrell, The Dangerous Goddess, *op. cit.*, p. 68.

5 Jill Low, 'The Art and Architectural Patronage of William Weddell (1736–92) of Newby Hall and his Circle', PhD thesis, Department of Fine Arts, University of Leeds, 1981, p.13.

6 Nineteen packing crates of antiquities, not including the Barberini Venus, for which export warrants were obtained in the following year on 27 March, 15 April and 17 May 1765: Adolf Michaelis, *Ancient Marbles in Great Britain*, Cambridge 1882, pp. 522–35.

7 Palgrave to Grant, 31 March 1765, quoted in Low thesis, *op. cit.*, 1981, p. 258

8 James Martin's unpublished manuscript diary of his Grand Tour, 1763–5, quoted in Ingamells, *A Dictionary of English and Irish Travellers in Italy, op. cit.*, p. 986–7.

9 *Ibid.* p. 986–7

10 Abbe Grant to James Grant, 26 June 1765, quoted in Ingamells, *op. cit.*, pp. 986–7.

11 Low thesis, *op. cit.*, 1981, p. 258.
12 WYAS (Leeds), VR 12411, Jenkins to Robinson, 5 June 1765.
13 Low thesis, *op. cit.*, p. 285. His patronage of British painters in Rome also echoed that of Grant and Robinson before him, Ingamells, *op. cit.*, p. 987.
14 Robin Middleton, 'The Sculpture Gallery at Newby Hall', *AA Files 13*, Autumn 1986, p. 60.
15 S. Rowland Pierce, 'Thomas Jenkins in Rome', *Journal of the Society of Antiquaries 45*, 1965, p. 219, fn. 4.
16 The Brutus was not found at Newby by the German scholar Adolf Michaelis in the nineteenth century, but it may have been subsequently identified as another character.
17 This sarcophagus or bath was a type of piece increasingly popular with English buyers towards the end of the century; for a similar example see Lord Darnley's Egyptian granite bath-tub sarcophagus at Cobham Hall, purchased c.1790: Cornelius C. Vermeule, *American Journal of Archaeology 59*, 1955, p.133. This piece was almost certainly supplied by Jenkins, from the evidence of payments from Darnley to Jenkins recorded by his bank: Coutts Bank Archives, The Strand, Ledger 97, (June 1789–June 1790) 456. Weddell's sarcophagus was eventually placed to form the focal point at the end of the vista in the gallery at Newby, (Figure 38) where its location was noted by Charles Townley in 1779; BM/TP, TY15/1/1, Sketch Plan of Newby, 1779.
18 Pierce, *op. cit.*, p. 219, fn. 4.
19 The conflicting accounts of various contemporary commentators are summarised in Michaelis, *op. cit.*, 1882, pp. 527–9; see also Jonathan Scott, *The Pleasures of Antiquity, British Collectors of Greece and Rome*, London, 2003, pp. 99–100.
20 Carlos A. Picon, *Bartolomeo Cavaceppi*, exhibition catalogue, Clarendon Gallery, London, 1983, pp. 48–51.
21 Michaelis, *op. cit.*, p. 528.
22 Barell, *op. cit.*, pp. 72-86.
23 Christie's International UK Ltd, catalogue, *The Jenkins Venus*, Thursday 13 June 2002
24 Eileen Harris, *The Genius of Robert Adam His Interiors*, New Haven and London, 2001, p. 218.
25 Howard Colvin, *A Biographical Dictionary of British Architects*, London, 1995, p. 54.
26 Middleton, *AA Files 13*, *op. cit.*, p. 50; see also Harris, *op. cit.*, pp. 215–8.
27 Palgrave prefaced a request for designs for a chimneypiece, 'What I really wish is to betake myself to your memory, that storehouse and repository of ancient and modern taste, and to beg of you by fancy and recollection to put together three or four ideas of elegance. . .' WYA, Rockingham Letters vol.2/3B, 66, Palgrave to Weddell, 12 May 1781.
28 WYAS (Leeds) WYL5013/D/1/6/2.
29 Middleton, *op. cit.*, p. 53; Harris, *op. cit.*, p. 216.
30 WYAS (Leeds) WYL5013/D/1/6/4, Newby Hall, Sculpture Gallery, Preliminary sketch for the rearrangement of the Sculpture Gallery, c.1767.
31 WYAS (Leeds) WYL109/Rockingham 2c, Palgrave to Weddell, 20 June c.1778: 'You go on, I trust, as brisk as bottled ale, with fresh delights rising every day about you. The gallery, I hope, draws very near its perfection. I look forward with great pleasure to the elegant breakfastings in the Portico, where Mrs. W. will sit and preside like another Aspasia, high arbitress and sovereign of the beaux arts'.
32 WYAS (Leeds) WYL5013/D/1/6/25 Newby Hall, Sculpture Gallery, no. 424, 'William Belwood. Full-size working drawing of pedestal'.
33 Middleton, *op. cit.*, p. 5. The subjects of 'Galleries' and 'Museums' were set several times between 1750–70 in the French Architectural Academy. Although none of the prize-winning solutions resembles the gallery at Newby closely, George Dance's design for a 'Public gallery for Statues, Pictures etc.', awarded the gold medal of the Parma Academy in 1763, offers a more complex solution using linked dome and rectangular spaces.
34 The coffering on the ceiling was taken from that in the Basilica of Maxentius, and that in the niches from the Temple of Venus and Rome: Kedleston House Archives, Lord Scarsdale, *Catalogue of the Pictures, Sculptures etc. at Kedleston, with some account of the Architecture*, (privately printed, 1770s with manuscript corrections c.1780), p. 4.
35 The Sir John Soane's Museum, Adam Drawings VII, pp. 200, 223–7. The designs are discussed in Alan A. Tait, *Robert Adam Drawings and Imagination*, Cambridge, 1993, pp. 84–7.
36 Eileen Harris and Nick Savage, *British Architectural Books and Writers 1556–1785*, Cambridge, 1990, p. 78.
37 Colvin, *op.cit.*, 1995, p. 54.
38 Thomas J. McCormick, *C. L. Clerisseau and the Genesis of Neo-Classicism*, New York and London, 1990, p. 50.
39 The Sir John Soane's Museum, Adam Drawings 56, 109.
40 McCormick, *op. cit.*, p. 180.
41 Richard Warner, *A Tour Through the Northern Counties of England, and the Borders of Scotland*, Bath, 1802, II, p. 254.
42 John Fleming, *Robert Adam and his Circle in Edinburgh and Rome*, London, 1962, pp. 203 and 208.
43 Adam's knowledge of Renaissance decoration was gleaned from sketching trips to the Palazzo Mattei, Palazzo Farnese, Villa Madama and Villa Papa Giulio with Clerisseau; Fleming, *op. cit.*, p. 203.
44 WYAS (Leeds) WYA, Rockingham Letters vol. 2A, p. 57: Lord Rockingham to Mr. Weddell, 12 August 1774.
45 Jenkins to James Grant, 5 June 1765, quoted in Ingamells, *op. cit.*, p. 987.
46 BM/TP, TY7/ 339, Jenkins to Townley, Rome, 19 October 1774.
47 BM/TP, TY7/ 359, Jenkins to Townley, Rome, 15 August 1776.
48 BM/TP, TY7/ 298, Jenkins to Townley, 9 November 1768.
49 BM/TP, TY7/297, Jenkins to Townley, 27 September 1768.
50 'I am glad you have got the cast of the Newby Goddess, and that it is so acceptable to you': BM/TP, TY7/301, Jenkins to Townley, 14 February 1770.
51 WYAS (Leeds) WYA L30/14/408/98, Robert Darley Waddilove to Grantham, 4 October 1779.
52 Low thesis, *op. cit.*, p. 264.
53 Michaelis, *op. cit.*, p. 428.
54 Picon, *op. cit.*, p. 50.
55 Low, *op. cit.*, p. 274.
56 The Sir John Soane's Museum, Adam Drawings, 41, 74: Plan of Newby Hall, undated.
57 Christopher Hussey, *English Country House, Mid-Georgian*, London, 1956, p. 144; see also Scott, *op. cit.*, pp. 133–4.
58 According to Thomas Jenkins, Weddell only proposed to visit Townley in 1779; he is also known to have asked to 'wait upon' Townley at Park Street with Mrs. Weddell in 1781: BM/TP, TY7/ 385, Jenkins to Townley, Rome 16 January 1779, BM/TP, TY7/1858, Weddell to Townley, 16 September 1781.
59 Dan Cruickshank, 'Queen Anne's Gate', *Georgian Group Journal*, 1992, pp. 65–6.
60 Ruth Guilding, *Marble Mania, Sculpture Galleries in England, 1640–1840*, Sir John Soane's Museum, 2001, pp. 42 and 45.
61 WYAS (Leeds) WYL 5013/2801/2, An Inventory of the Statues, Busts and fixtures at Newby Hall, 25th May 1794.

62 BM/TP, TY7/385, Jenkins to Townley, Rome, 16 January 1779.

63 BM/TP, TY7/ 385, Jenkins to Townley, Castel Gandolfo, 15 July 1779.

64 BM/TP, TY3/6-11, Correspondence between the Adam brothers and Charles Townley, London, 1777–9.

65 Joseph Bonomi, Design for a Sculpture gallery at Towneley Hall for Charles Townley, c.1783–90 (private collection). See also Guilding, *op. cit.*, 2002, p. 42

66 WYAS (Leeds) WYL5013/D/2801/2.

67 BM/TP, TY15/1/1, Sketch plan of the gallery at Newby.

68 BM/TP, TY15/1/1, Sketch plan of Newby, 1779.

69 WYAS (Leeds) WYL 5013/D/2801/2.

70 BM/TP, TY7/ 385, Jenkins to Townley, Rome, 16 January 1779.

71 The Ibis was illustrated in volume 1 of Bartolomeo Cavaceppi's *Raccolta d'antiche Statue*, (1768) having passed through his restoration workshops, Michaelis, *op. cit.*, 1882, p. 534.

72 Two marble groups of Lions attacking Buffaloes are among pieces listed in the 4th Earl of Carlisle's Probate Inventory of 1759: Castle Howard Archives, F4/1, Inventory of Household Furniture. . . Rt. Hon. Earl of Carlisle, 1759.

73 Another figure of a baboon, formerly in the Villa Mattei (and illustrated in the *Raccolte*, III (1772), mounted upon the second of the two pedestals acquired by Weddell) was bought by Thomas Blundell for his gallery at Ince. Thomas Blundell, Andrew Wilton and Ilaria Bignamini, eds., *Grand Tour, The Lure of Italy in the Eighteenth Century*, Tate Gallery, London, 1996, pp. 306–7. Townley acquired a group of two dogs from excavations by Gavin Hamilton at Monte Cagnolo in 1774, and a second group was acquired from him in the same year for the Museo Pio-Clementino, and later displayed in the Sala degli Animali there, opened in 1782 to draw together a large array of animal pieces both newly and anciently acquired: Wilton and Bignamini, *op. cit.*, 1996, pp. 250–1.

74 Gervase Jackson-Stops (ed.), *The Treasure Houses of Great Britain, Five Hundred Years of Private Patronage and Art Collecting*, London, 1985, p. 306.

75 Michaelis, *op. cit.*, p. 531.

76 Pierce, *JSA 45, op. cit.*, p. 217.

77 Jackson-Stops, ed., *op. cit.*, p. 310.

78 'Views of the Past: Reflections on the Treatment of Historical Objects and Museums of History', in Stephen Bann, *The Inventions of History, Essays on the Representation of the Past*, Manchester, 1990, p. 135.

79 Thomas Mulvany, *The Life of James Gandon Esq*, London, 1969, pp. 197–8.

80 WYA, Rockingham letters vol. 2A, p.57, Rockingham to Weddell, 12 August 1774.

81 Edward R. Mayor, 'The Sculpture Collection of the Second Marquis of Rockingham at Wentworth Woodhouse', MPhil. thesis, Sheffield Hallam University, 1987, pp. 10–11.

82 John Brewer, 'A Most Polite Age and the Most Vicious Attitudes towards Culture as a Commodity, 1660–1800', in Ann Bermingham and John Brewer, eds., *The Consumption of Culture 1600–1800, Image, Object, Text*, London, 1995, p. 350.

83 C. B. Cone, 'Edmund Burke's Art Collection', *Art Bulletin XXIX*, 1947, p. 126–31.

84 Barrell, *op. cit.*, pp. 63 and 70.

85 WYAS (Leeds) WYL109/Rockingham 2c, Palgrave to Weddell, 20 June 1778.

86 Low, *op. cit.*, pp. 20, 25.

87 *Ibid.* p. 28.

88 WYAS (Leeds) R.A. 2c.64, Weddell to his wife, 13 December 1788.

89 WYAS (Leeds) Ramsden Mss.80–88, Burke to Weddell, 31 January 1792.

90 Nollekens had sculpted Weddell's bust c.1771–5, this copy is dated 1795.

91 Low, *op. cit.*, p.41.

92 The monument enclosed his statue by Nollekens dated 1774 and the busts of eight of his supporters.

93 Memorial on the funerary monument to Weddell in Ripon Cathedral.

94 WYAS (Leeds) Ra 2c.92, Tribute anonymously sent to Mrs. Weddell on her husband's death.